A Student's Guide to Volunteering

A Student's Guide to Volunteering

By
Theresa Foy DiGeronimo

CAREER PRESS
3 Tice Road
P.O. Box 687
Franklin Lakes, NJ 07417
1-800-CAREER-1
201-848-0310 (outside U.S.)
FAX: 201-848-1727

A STUDENT'S GUIDE TO VOLUNTEERING

ISBN 1-56414-170-5, $10.99

Cover design by The Visual Group

Printed in the U.S.A. by Book-mart Press

To order this title by mail, please include price as noted above, $2.50 handling per order, and $1.00 for each book ordered. Send to: Career Press, Inc., 3 Tice Road, P.O. Box 687, Franklin Lakes, NJ 07417

Or call toll-free 1-800-CAREER-1 (Canada: 201-848-0310) to order using VISA or MasterCard, or for further information on books from Career Press.

Library of Congress Cataloging-in-Publication Data

DiGeronimo, Theresa Foy.
A student's guide to volunteering / by Theresa DiGeronimo.
p. cm.
Includes index.
ISBN 1-56414-170-5 : $10.99
1. Student service--United States. 2. Student volunteers in social service--United States. 3. Associations, institutions, etc.--United States--Directories. I. Title.
LC220.5.D54 1995
361.3'7--dc20 95-6283
CIP

Dedication

I dedicate this book to my children, Matt, Joe and Colleen, with the hope that they will grow up to give of themselves in the volunteer spirit of dedication and love that will make the world a better place for us all.

Acknowledgments

I would like to thank my staff of four who tirelessly made phone calls, culled libraries, interviewed volunteers and organized reams of information into workable form:

- Matt DiGeronimo for his late-night editorial efforts on the chapters focusing on protecting the environment and politics.
- Domenick Stampone for his thorough work on the chapter dealing with education.
- Mary Shumeyko for her expertise and invaluable contribution to the chapter on starting your own volunteer program and the teen story illustrating substance abuse prevention.
- Terry Coyle for his much-appreciated assistance in formulating the chapters on the needy and substance abuse prevention.

And of course, I'd like to thank all the teens who contributed their stories. It's their adventures that bring the lure of volunteering to life.

Contents

A Student's Guide to Volunteering

Chapter One	Everybody's Doing It!	9
Chapter Two	Health Care	17
Chapter Three	Substance Abuse Prevention	33
Chapter Four	The Needy	49
Chapter Five	Education	63
Chapter Six	Protecting the Environment	79
Chapter Seven	Politics	95
Chapter Eight	Doing It Yourself	109
Epilogue		125
Directory		127
About the Author		179
Index		181

Chapter One

Everybody's Doing It!

It's true! America is built on the backs of 94 million people like you who are willing to volunteer their time and talent. This isn't just a pat-on-the-back compliment—it's a fact. The volunteer efforts of today's Americans are worth $176 billion dollars. If people didn't offer their services freely without expecting money, this country would fall to pieces. Without the goodwill of volunteers, many Americans would die of starvation, thousands of addicts left for dead, illiterates ignored, poor unclothed, rivers polluted, museums unopened, theaters closed, children neglected, mentally ill uncomforted, elderly abandoned and schools and churches shut down. Welcome to the volunteer movement that keeps this country going.

A little history

We can't even imagine a country without volunteers because, from its earliest days, America has counted on those who lend a hand. At first, during the Colonial period, this neighborly banding together for a common cause was necessary for survival. Then during the Civil War in the mid-1800s, there was a shift from individual volunteerism to organized group activities. During this time many of the organizations we today associate with volunteer work were organized, including: the Red Cross, Young Men's Christian Association (YMCA), American branch of the Salvation Army, the National Tuberculosis Association, Boys Clubs, the National Society for the Prevention of Blindness, the National Association for Mental Health, Boy Scouts, Goodwill Industries and the American Cancer Society.

During World War I and then again in the Depression, organized volunteerism grew and matured. At this time there was a drastic change in attitude that took volunteer service out of the hands of the upper class and spread the work through middle-class America.

Then in the 1960s, a new kind of volunteerism rose out of the work of young student activists. These young adults turned their attention to political causes and to the quest for world peace. This generation of idealistic volunteers demonstrated the tremendous will and dedication young people have to offer.

In their footsteps have followed the 10 million high school and college students who today volunteer their time and talent each year.

10 million young adult volunteers!

Can you image how many 10 million really is? Well, picture this: If you stood each of these young volunteers shoulder-to-shoulder in a straight line across this country, they would easily reach from Los Angeles, California, to New York City. This picture certainly tells more about your generation than the daily headlines. Too often the media blares the bad news of violence and crime among a generation accused of being a selfish group looking for instant gratification. The fact that you're reading this book is proof that the unselfish charity that built this country is in no danger of dying out.

What are all these young adults doing? Consider these examples:

- Young people founded a natural science museum in upstate New York.
- Kids built a community playground in Dade County, Florida.
- YES (Youth Elderly Services) kids in Fall River, Massachusetts, formed a group that provides companionship for the elderly in nursing homes.
- Teens man hotline phones to talk with others their own age who are in trouble; HAIR (Help and Information Resource) in Battle Creek, Michigan, and Metro-help in Chicago, Illinois, are examples of such hotline agencies.
- CRUD (Citizens for Recycling and Usage of Disposables) is a teen-organized ecology program in Beverly Hills, California.
- For the past 10 years, Students of Hawthorne Acting Responsibly and Effectively (SHARE) in suburban New Jersey has sponsored food and clothing drives and hosted holiday parties for a nearby needy urban school district.
- The Student Conservation Association, Inc., of Vashon, Washington, enables students to volunteer in national parks repairing trails, building bridges, putting up fences and acting as tour guides.

These are just a few examples of what's going on. Today, more than any other time, young volunteers are giving of themselves and making a difference. Their efforts are being recorded in magazines like *Newsweek, Time, U.S. News & World Report, Phi Delta Kappan* and *National Geographic World*. Their work is receiving attention and being applauded on network TV news shows and in daily papers. The word is out: Youth volunteerism is *in*!

What kind of teens volunteer?

When you make a mental picture of a volunteer, what does he or she look like? What kind of person volunteers? What are his or her interests and hobbies? Although you might have a mental image of a volunteer worker, the truth is: No one picture is absolutely correct. America's 500,000 volunteer agencies receive help, support and power from individuals who mirror the unique tapestry of America itself.

Volunteers are everyone—rich and poor and everything in-between. They are male and female. They live in cities, in suburbs, on farms and in ghettos. They are good students, poor students and dropouts. They come from two-parent homes, single-parent homes, foster homes, group homes and detention homes. And they are from every ethnic background, race and religion that exists in our country.

Why volunteer?

Although no two volunteers are exactly alike, *all* volunteers share two absolutely necessary attributes: caring and the resolve to make things better.

And while these attributes are important, there are lots of other reasons students decide to volunteer. Consider these:

Build impressive credentials. Jake wants to get accepted at a university veterinary school. Maggie wants to get a job at a prestigious accounting firm after her college graduation. So, both Jake and Maggie are volunteering their skills to make sure their applications look good. For the last year, Jake has volunteered two hours every Saturday morning at the city's animal shelter. And every March and April for the last two years, Maggie has helped senior citizens prepare their income tax returns.

Gain career experience. Roberta thinks she wants to be a lawyer. She spends two afternoons a week answering phones, filing, typing and running errands for the city public defender's office. Even though she doesn't want to be a law clerk, her time in the office gives her a chance to watch lawyers in action. This insider's view is helping Roberta decide if law is the field for her.

Jesse is absolutely sure he wants to be a psychologist. By volunteering to be an on-call peer listener, he is learning a lot about human behavior and feelings. Jesse's phone number is listed in a directory that's given to all his high school classmates. Anyone can call him anytime about any kind of problem, and Jesse is there to listen. Jesse believes this experience will help him when his professional training begins.

Roberta and Jesse will be glad to learn that many employers, including federal and state governments, will accept their volunteer experience as part of their work history.

Share a personal interest. Tanya loves to draw. Kevin is a talented drummer. Both of these students share their talent with disadvantaged children at a nearby day-care center. The kids love the extra attention Tanya and Kevin give them, and they're also learning about art and music. That's something these teen volunteers know would not be a part of the children's lives if it weren't for their willingness to share what they love.

Meet people with similar interests. Thomas is very interested in politics, but none of his school friends share his interest. In fact, most of them don't even know the names of the candidates in state and local elections. Last summer, Thomas joined a group of people who were campaigning for a congressional candidate. Thomas made phone calls, put up posters, attended rallies and distributed literature. Although he certainly helped the campaign, for Thomas the real reward was in making many new friends who shared his interest in politics.

Relieve boredom. Michele dreaded her upcoming spring break. Many of her college friends were going away on exciting vacations; others were working; and the rest were going home to distant states. There would be nothing to do.

Then Michele heard about a relief drive being organized to help people in a neighboring state whose homes were destroyed by a recent hurricane. Without a second thought, Michele offered to jump on a bus filled with volunteers armed with hammers and nails. She was glad to spend her spring vacation putting houses and lives back together. Not only did this mission help Michele avoid the boredom she expected would plague her spring break, she felt good about spending her time helping others.

Fulfill school requirements. Marc is the star of his high school basketball team. His school work, sport practices, games and a part-time job keep him very busy. So, in the beginning, he was not at all happy about the idea of having to put in community service time. But because it was a graduation requirement, Marc agreed to spend one hour every Saturday morning at the local Boys Club helping kids learn how to play basketball.

The payback

If some of these reasons for volunteering seem self-serving, that's because they are—but that's okay. When volunteers go into service wanting to gain some specific goal, they usually end up giving and getting more than they originally expected.

You can think of the process of volunteering like an investment. You invest your time and talent in carefully measured amounts, but after awhile the return on your investment grows. When that happens, the reasons for volunteering often change. What starts out as a way to meet friends, relieve boredom or meet school requirements often grows into a heartfelt love of the job. This is when the rewards really multiply.

Volunteering offers the best opportunity to expand your horizons beyond your small group of friends and family. It gives you experiences and knowledge that make you a better person. Volunteering can give you a chance to grow and mature emotionally and intellectually. Volunteer service is a special source of personal satisfaction. It is an opportunity to learn new skills, gain new insights and achieve a sense of accomplishment. Being useful and helpful gives us something we all can use—a good feeling. And as a bonus, it's fun and it builds a better society for us all.

The volunteer personality

Millions of young adults volunteer to make this country a better place. But some volunteer efforts make a more lasting impression on the quality of life than others. Why is that? Well, for starters, it has something to do with what can be called the "volunteer personality." The teens who make a difference often possess these traits:

- **A desire for challenge and responsibility**: Volunteers are often expected to do challenging work without close supervision.
- **Enthusiasm**: Attitude is everything!

- **Common sense**: Volunteers need to know good from bad and right from wrong. Without this knowledge, it's easy to go over the line from helping to hurting.
- **Personal interest in the area of work**: Volunteering shouldn't be a chore—make it something you enjoy.
- **Ingenuity**: Problem-solving is often a component of volunteer work.
- **Compassion**: The disadvantaged don't want to feel that they owe you a debt of gratitude. Volunteer aid is offered with no strings attached.
- **Team spirit**: Volunteers work as a group for the good of the community and the organization; there's no room for super egos.

No one person can be all these things all the time. But this list gives you an idea of the characteristics that will help you get the most out of your volunteer experience.

What really counts

You may start out volunteering for any number of personal reasons. You may possess some or all of the "volunteer personality" traits. You may be forced to volunteer or you may be driven by a real desire to do good. But always remember: In the end, anyone who cares and is willing to do something about that caring *can* make a difference.

The following chapters will guide you, step-by-step, through your adventure in volunteering. Good luck!

Chapter Two

Health Care

There are more than 6,000 hospitals in the United States and even more clinics, rehabilitation centers, outpatient facilities, homes for the elderly, disabled and mentally handicapped, and private health organizations that need your help. In fact, the health-care field offers teenagers more volunteer opportunities than any other area of service.

Why do it?

There are hundreds of reasons you might want to volunteer in the health-care field. Some teens have said:

- *"I want to be a nurse, and I think this will look good on my resume."*

- *"I like helping other people."*
- *"A friend of mine was killed, and I decided I wanted to do something for patients and their family and friends so they won't have to go through what I went through."*
- *"I started because my friends were doing it for a school project, but when they were finished, I continued because I found out I really like working with sick children."*
- *"My mom thought it would be good for me."*
- *"I never thought I'd want to volunteer. But one day I went with my friend to visit her grandmother in a nursing home. I found out I really liked visiting with older people, so now I go once a week."*
- *"I want to do something in the medical field, but I'm not sure what. Being in the hospital is helping me decide what I want to do—and what I don't want to do."*
- *"I never even thought about a career in medicine until I started volunteering. Now I know I definitely want to be a surgeon—I just have to decide what kind of surgeon!"*

What it takes

Whatever your reason for thinking about volunteering in the health-care field, there are certain personality traits that will help you make a success of your efforts. Teen volunteers in the health-care field generally have these characteristics:

- They have a special compassion for the ill.
- They aren't squeamish about pain and disease.
- They aren't judgmental toward the elderly, disabled or mentally infirm.
- They can deal with death and loss.
- They are responsible and committed.
- They know how to follow orders.
- They can work as part of a team.

Robin Cox, a 17-year-old who volunteers at a home for the elderly, agrees that all of these things are important. She also adds: "I think it's real important when you work with ill or elderly people that you have lots of patience and that you're a good conversationalist and a good listener."

Who's allowed?

Both male and female volunteers are needed in the health-care industry. Each organization will have its own eligibility requirements, but in general you'll need to be over the age of 13 and in good health. Some places will require that you have a complete physical before beginning your service; others may want only verification of TB and rubella inoculation. Some may have no health requirements at all. Whatever the health requirements, if you deal directly with patients, you probably won't be able to work on days when you have a cold, sore throat, temperature or rash.

If you are under legal age, you will also need your parent or guardian's written permission.

Can you keep a secret?

Like doctors, nurses and other medical professionals, as a health-care volunteer you are bound by a code of ethics. Perhaps the most important is the issue of confidentiality.

It is very important to respect a patient's right to privacy. Information about any patient, illness or treatment should never be discussed or repeated inside or outside the medical facility. You should not even ask a patient the reason he or she is ill. You should not talk about your own medical problems, and you must never attempt to give advice or give your opinion about a diagnosis or treatment. Health-care volunteers must be mature enough to keep quiet.

Hospital volunteers

In the typical hospital setting, volunteers are needed many places. Most assign volunteers to places on the following list.

Patient contact assignments. If you like to work directly with patients, most hospitals allow junior volunteers to work in these areas:

- **Admitting**. You can sign in patients as they arrive at the hospital and direct them to the place where they should go.
- **Dietary**. You will distribute and collect meal menus. You may help some patients read and fill out the menu forms.
- **Hospitality gift cart**. You go from room to room asking patients if they would like to buy anything from your cart. Items for sale may include magazines, books, crossword puzzles, newspapers, breath mints, toothpaste, combs and the like.
- **Mail and flower delivery**. Naturally, an enormous amount of get-well wishes arrive at a hospital every day. Volunteers help deliver the mail and flowers to the patients' rooms.
- **Various nursing units**. Each unit in the hospital centers around the nurses' station. Volunteers may be assigned to a particular station to help the nurses with a variety of tasks like making beds, feeding patients and filling water pitchers.
- **Radiology host or hostess**. As patients arrive at the radiology department, volunteers help them follow the sign-in procedure.
- **Recovery room**. Some volunteers assist patients coming out of anesthesia in the recovery room. Volunteers may give blankets to patients who feel cold, ice to those who are thirsty and words of comfort to those who are frightened.
- **Transport**. After learning how to use wheelchairs properly and safely, volunteers may be asked to move patients from one place to another.

Services to visitors. You may be needed to help visitors who come to the hospital. A volunteer assignment in this area may include working at the information desk where you answer questions and give directions. Volunteers also help visitors by working behind the counter in the hospital gift shops and cafeteria.

Assistance to hospital staff. In some cases you may be needed to help the hospital staff. These positions are often in:

- **The mailroom**. Before mail is delivered to the patients, volunteers in the mailroom sort it out according to floor and/or unit.
- **Child-care center**. Some hospitals offer child-care for their employees. Volunteers can work with these children in the child-care center.
- **Laboratory**. Volunteers usually run errands and act as messengers in this department.
- **Sewing room**. Many hospitals ask volunteers to help them mend hospital gowns, pillowcases, sheets and so on.
- **Clerical**. Hospitals need secretaries and receptionists. At a hospital you may be needed to help answer phones and complete and/or file paperwork in any one of the many departments.

As you can see, volunteers are very much needed in hospitals. Most volunteer programs allow you to choose the area you'd like to work in and to change your mind and move to another area of service if you'd like.

Get ready to do time

Because hospitals have such a large volunteer work force, their programs tend to be very organized and structured around sincere commitment. Although volunteers aren't paid, the patients and the staff depend on them. Catherine McMullen, director of volunteer services at a private suburban hospital, says, "We accept teens who want to volunteer for at least 40 hours, because much training is needed. We require a pledge to these minimum number of hours before we'll accept an application." Most hospitals have a minimum time commitment for their volunteers, but they're not all the same. One may ask for at least four hours a week for a total of five weeks; another may ask for a minimum of 75 hours spread over one school year. When you begin to look into the possibility of volunteering at a hospital, be sure to ask about the required time commitment.

On your best behavior

A hospital setting puts you in the public's eye as a representative of the hospital. That's why most hospitals ask their volunteers to abide by a code of conduct. You will probably be given a written list of do's and don'ts that will include instructions like:

- Don't chew gum, eat or read while on duty.
- Don't sit on a patient's bed.
- Don't ask a doctor or nurse for medical advice while on duty.
- Do show a cheerful, kind and sympathetic attitude.
- Do take directions and criticism willingly.

These, and others like them, aren't terribly difficult requests, but they are important to the image of the hospital and junior volunteers must be willing to follow certain rules of conduct.

Learning the ropes

Before you begin your volunteer service, you will be given some sort of introduction to the volunteer program and the hospital itself. At an orientation, you'll learn the guidelines of conduct, dress, emergency codes, fire safety and infection control procedures. Generally, you also take a tour of the hospital to learn where everything is, and you learn how to transport patients in wheelchairs (a common job of volunteers).

A senior volunteer, a staff person or a nurse will teach you the tasks you'll be asked to do in your assigned area of work. You might, for example, learn how to feed elderly or disabled patients and how to make beds.

In some hospitals, orientation and training for volunteers is finished in a one-hour meeting, and in others it's an ongoing program that meets every few weeks.

Staying healthy

As you think about volunteering in the health-care field, you and your family may wonder about the risk of catching an infectious disease; some families are especially concerned about being exposed to HIV/AIDS. Most hospital personnel understand your concern and will arm you with the facts and preventative measures that will put an end to your fears.

You will learn about "universal precautions." These are special measures meant to be observed universally—in *all* hospitals by *all* caregivers for *all* patients. They're designed to protect both caregivers and patients from the spread of a bloodborne disease like HIV or Hepatitis B. Universal precautions are used by volunteers when performing tasks such as disposing of garbage. Gloves, gowns, masks and/or eye protectors may be required.

The extent of the precautions you'll use depends upon the type of contact you have with patients and the type of care you provide. In any case, you should be trained in all tasks that involve patient care. Even changing bed linen or delivering blood samples to the lab can be risky if you don't know how to do it properly.

Most hospitals make sure their volunteers are fully trained in infection control, but if you should ever be asked to do a job that requires direct contact with a patient or his or her things, don't hesitate to ask for an explanation. The staff person who made the request may assume that someone else has taught you the proper technique. Don't be afraid to speak up and clearly admit, "I don't know how." Then ask, "Will you show me?"

Uniforms!

All hospital volunteers wear some kind of uniform. Some hospitals still require girls to wear the traditional "candystriper" pink-and-white-striped pinafore with white blouse and white shoes, and they require boys to wear a jacket and tie. Others have given up the formal look and have moved to a uniform T-shirt designed with the hospital volunteer program logo worn with white or dark-colored pants. For safety reasons volunteers wear low-heeled shoes (preferably with rubber soles) with stockings or socks. No sandals, clogs or boots are allowed.

Sometimes the hospital gives you the uniform, but most often the volunteer must buy it.

Whatever the type uniform, you are responsible for wearing it every time you are on duty and for keeping it neat and clean.

Many hospitals also have rules about accessories and appearance. You may be asked not to wear overpowering perfume or cologne, hats, anything but the most basic jewelry and any hairstyle that gets in your way.

Recognition and rewards

Hospitals generally have a program of service awards that are given after completing a certain number of volunteer hours. One hospital, for example, awards service stripes that are worn on the uniform after the volunteer has completed 30, 60 and 100 hours. After 150 hours of service, junior volunteers are eligible for the hospital's volunteer service pin. Other special awards are presented at 500, 750 and 1,000 hours of service. Additional recognition is given at volunteer receptions and ceremonies held throughout the year. Most hospitals have some kind of reward system.

Although these pins of recognition are nice, most junior volunteers take home other awards that are much more special to them:

"The reward isn't a material thing I can grasp. It's a feeling that I can't really describe. But it makes me feel good, and I think it's a feeling all volunteers get."

—Angela Yap, 19

Angela began volunteering four years ago at her local hospital. Today she's a pre-med student at college and volunteers at a hospital clinic for homeless and battered women.

"I keep coming because I'm learning a lot about medicine. By the time I finish high school, I'll know if I want to be a doctor."

—Sergio Valente, 14

Sergio has just finished his first summer as a hospital youth volunteer.

"It's hard to describe what I get out of this; a lot of my friends say I should get a real job. But when people who are so sick or are in pain smile at me and remember me when they see me again, I feel great."

—Laura Capone, 18

Laura just finished her first summer of volunteering at an adult day-care facility for the elderly.

"I like it here because I meet a lot of different people—patients, other volunteers and even the staff."

—Schevone Johnson, 14

Schevone has worked as a hospital volunteer for more than a year and is trying to decide between a career in pediatrics or engineering.

"I like to work in the Alzheimer's unit even though most of the people there don't remember me from one day to the next. But once in a while something happens that reminds me why I like to be there. I remember there was a man named Hanz who had been at Auschwitz and would sometimes have flashbacks. One day I was walking down the hall after I'd been away for two weeks, and I heard someone call my name. 'Robin! Robin, come here.' It was Hanz. I couldn't believe he remembered me. It felt so good to be somebody he remembered and missed while I was gone. It's these kind of experiences that give me a lot of self-confidence and really bring out the best in me and just make me happy."

—Robin Cox, 17

Robin has volunteered her time at a residential home for the elderly for two years.

Getting started

If you decide you'd like to volunteer at a hospital, it's really quite easy to get started. If there is a local hospital you'd like to work in, just call the main number and ask for the volunteer services department.

If you're not sure where you can find a hospital with a good volunteer program, you can call the American Hospital Association, Division of Volunteer Services. A representative will refer you to a junior volunteer program near your home. Call the Chicago headquarters: 312-280-6000.

If you live near several hospitals, take advantage of your good luck by finding the one that best fits your needs. Call each hospital and ask them to send you information about their junior volunteer program. Then compare! How many hours a week does each require?

What kind of uniform does each have and who pays for it? Can you choose where you will work? Does the hospital offer college scholarships to their junior volunteers? Think about what's important to you before you sign up. Get all the facts that will help you decide where you'd like to volunteer.

Other medical facilities

Although hospitals are by far the most popular places for junior volunteers, there are many other health facilities that welcome the time and talent of teenagers. From personal experience with a health problem, you may know of a clinic or rehabilitation center that could use your help. Or, if a family member or friend has a particular disease or condition, you may be familiar with the need for volunteers in that area. Opportunities are all around us—the American Red Cross, the March of Dimes, the National Multiple Sclerosis Society and many, many others need volunteer helpers. Usually a simple phone call is all it takes to find out if teen volunteers are welcome.

The list of health-related organizations in the Directory will give you an idea of the many places where you can help out.

A bad match

Sometimes volunteering in the health-care field turns out to be a bad experience because the teen just doesn't fit in the medical environment. One junior volunteer remembers working with a boy who had to put in 25 hours of community service to graduate high school. "He hated every minute of his time on duty. This kid would work eight hours straight on a weekend just to get it over with. But I don't think he had a problem with the fact that he had to volunteer; I think it was just the hospital environment that bothered him."

Sometimes this happens and it's nothing to feel bad about. There are plenty of other fields of service where you can find a better match for your skills and the community's needs.

But other times the bad experience isn't because the teen is poorly suited to the health-care field; it's just that he or she ended up in the wrong area of health care. If you don't like your first volunteer job, take some advice from these volunteers:

> *"I started out in the child-care center the hospital has for its employees, but I didn't like that. After the first week, I asked if I could be moved into the hospital itself, and that's when I got interested in medicine. Now I'm in the pre-med volunteer program that lets me do even more than the regular junior volunteers."*

> *"First I volunteered in another hospital. I didn't like it there at all; mostly I didn't like the attitude of the staff. They acted like they didn't want me around, and they wouldn't let me do anything. So I quit after about two weeks, and then the next summer I tried another hospital. I have to drive a little farther to get here, but I'm glad I didn't give up completely because I really love it now."*

> *"I volunteered at a private health organization, and it was real boring. All I did was stuff envelopes and answer the phone. I think I'd like working directly with people, so now I'm looking for some place else that will be more challenging for me."*

Volunteering in the health-care field can be a very challenging and rewarding experience. Let's take a peek at the typical activities a hospital volunteer might encounter.

A day in the life of two hospital volunteers: Corrine and Annamarie

It's 8:00 Saturday morning on the last weekend of the summer when Corrine Wallace and her good friend Annamarie Nesci arrive for duty. These two 14-year-olds volunteer every weekend at the courtesy desk of a small Catholic hospital. Like the day itself, on this morning the hospital is brightly lit but still sleepy. Corrine pulls her extra-large sweatshirt closer to her body. "It's cold this morning," she shivers. "I can't believe I'm going to start high school next week. The summer went by so fast."

"Yeah," agrees Annamarie, turning on the radio that sits in the corner of the volunteer services office, which will serve as the girl's home base for the next four hours. "Some days, it's so busy we get crazy and the time really flies." The girls laugh when they remember how Corrine's hair was flying all over the place the week before when she came racing down the hall after trying to do three jobs at one time. "You looked a mess!" kids Annamarie. "But other days, like this one, it's pretty slow and we can talk or read, or even do homework."

It's easy to see why Corrine and Annamarie enjoy their work. Volunteers at the courtesy desk are on call to run errands for staff members anywhere in the hospital. As soon as the phone rings, the girls know they're needed.

Rrrrring... The first call of the day asks for help discharging a patient. Leaving Corrine in the office to answer the phone, Annamarie pulls hair into a ponytail, takes a wheelchair from its space against the wall and then goes off to bring a patient from the hospital room to the front exit. (Sometimes, like today, the wheelchairs are parked in their spaces and ready for use, but on other days, the girls' first task is to round up stray chairs.) Annamarie expertly maneuvers the chair through the hallways, onto the elevator and up to the sixth floor. In Room 607 an elderly woman stands when she sees the wheelchair and then takes one last look around the room to make sure she hasn't left anything behind.

"Hi," says Annamarie brightly. "Ready to go?" Without response, the woman sits in the wheelchair and her son places her flower arrangement on her lap. The balloons stretching up from the flowers bounce against Annamarie's face, making it difficult to see as she heads down the hall.

"Oh, I'm sorry," says the woman as she looks back and sees Annamarie trying to dodge the balloons and find the elevator button. Lowering the balloons to her lap, the woman laughs and seems to relax a bit. "Thank you for the ride," she says. "You're welcome," says Annamarie flashing her always-ready smile. Once outside, the woman and her son again thank Annamarie as they get into a waiting car. "Most people are really nice here," remarks Annamarie. "Sometimes they even give me a tip, but that money gets turned back to the hospital."

Back at the courtesy desk, Corrine has gotten another call. Someone from the kitchen wanted her to pick up a tray of canned liquid nutrient and bring it to the intensive care unit. Annamarie knows where her friend has gone, because every call is recorded in a book on the desk. As soon as she gets back to the office, Annamarie checks the book then sits down to wait for her next call. "I really like it here," she says. "No two days are alike—you never know who'll call next or what they'll need. If I were at home I'd probably sleep until noon so I'm not missing anything by being here."

Rrrrring... "Courtesy desk. Annamarie speaking." As she finishes jotting down the instructions, Corrine walks in. "Oh good. You're just in time," smirks Annamarie. "How'd you like to go down to the laundry and pick up clean linens for the emergency room?"

"Oh, thanks," Corrine shoots back. "Okay. But you take the next two calls."

Corrine navigates her way through the corridor maze and down to the basement laundry room. "The hardest part of volunteering at first," she remembers, "was finding my way around. For the first three weeks I needed somebody to come with me on every errand. Now that I've been here for more than a year, I know where almost every department is—but sometimes I still get a little lost." The linens are stacked and waiting for Corrine. So she loads up her arms and begins the return trip.

Mission accomplished, Corrine joins Annamarie back at the desk. Passing the time during a slow period, the two trade tales of their most memorable volunteer assignments. "I will never forget the time I got a call to take a pregnant woman from the emergency room (we call it the ER) to the labor and delivery unit," starts Corrine. "She was moaning and yelling, and I knew I should hurry, but I couldn't find a wheelchair anywhere. Finally, she insisted on going without a wheelchair. So there we are walking down the hall, just the two of us, and the whole time I'm praying, 'Please don't let her have this baby right now. I'm only 14 and I'm not supposed to see things like that!' Then we got on the elevator and she started moaning again. I quickly looked for the emergency phone and the alarm in case the elevator got stuck and she started to have the baby. We finally made it to the maternity floor okay. But that was the longest trip from the ER to labor and delivery I've ever taken!"

"I remember when that happened," gasps Annamarie almost crying from laughing so hard.

"Well, what about the time you brought that baby and her mother up to surgery?" says Corrine pointing her finger at Annamarie. "You didn't do much better."

"Oh, yeah, I remember that. I got a call from the admitting office to show a patient to the same-day surgical unit. So I go down there and there's this mother holding a tiny baby. The mother is crying so hard it looks like her eyes are bleeding. I tell her to follow me and as we walk through the hospital, this mother is sobbing the whole way. I didn't know what to do or say and then I started to cry. I felt so sorry for her. I think when we got to the surgical unit I said something like, 'I'm sure everything will be all right.' But I felt awful. That's just the way I am; I cry very easily, especially if somebody else is hurting."

Rrrrring... "Courtesy Desk. Annamarie speaking." Annamarie hangs up the phone, jots her assignment in the log and then heads for the wheelchair. "There's a discharge in pediatrics," she tells Corrine. "I'll go; I like bringing out little kids." Full of confidence, Annamarie makes her way to the pediatric floor.

Soon she passes through the large wooden doors that separate the standard hospital hallways of white walls and floors from the colorful pediatric halls wallpapered with dancing bears and balloons. Down at the end of the corridor, Annamarie finds Room 411 and turns in looking for her littlest patient of the day. There, waiting for her, sits a large teenage boy with his entire head wrapped in gauze protecting some seemingly awful head wound.

Hiding her surprise, Annamarie offers the boy a ride to the front door, and his mother follows close behind. The trip to the exit is long and silent. No one speaks a word. "Sometimes you can just tell that a patient doesn't want to talk," says Annamarie as the young man and his mother leave the hospital parking lot.

It's clear that on this job you can never be sure what's going to be around the next corner. This proves true as Annamarie waits for the elevator on her return to the volunteer office. Down the hall races a team of nurses pushing a stretcher toward the elevator. On the stretcher is a very old and very pale man with an IV line in his arm and an oxygen tube in his mouth. The team is in a hurry and Annamarie steps aside to let them use the elevator. Even though youth volunteers aren't involved in the direct care of seriously ill patients, it is, after all, a hospital and they do see a lot of illness and suffering.

Catching the next elevator, Annamarie finally gets back to the office as Corrine is hanging up the phone. "The nurses in ER want two coffees with milk and sugar," she tells Annamarie. The girls say that sometimes these kinds of personal errands can be annoying, especially if they're really busy. But right now things are slow and these nurses are always nice, so they don't mind doing them a favor. Besides, it's time for a break anyway. "I'll go with you," says Annamarie, "and then we'll have lunch."

Each day they work, the volunteers are given meal tickets worth $5 in the hospital cafeteria. Annamarie and Corrine deliver the coffee to the ER and then head toward the cafeteria for a half-hour break.

Over lunch the girls think about their future as hospital volunteers. "As soon as I turn 16," says Annamarie, "I can pick a special field I want to volunteer in. I know I want to be a physical therapist when I grow up, so I'm going to keep volunteering here so I can work in the physical therapy department. That will be good experience, and it will look good on my college applications because physical therapy is real hard to get into."

"I'm going to keep volunteering here all through high school because I like it," says Corrine. "And I've heard that the hospital gives out college scholarships to some volunteers; that would really help my family. As soon as I can, I'm going to get a job to earn money, but I'll still volunteer. I think I could volunteer here on

Saturday mornings and still have any other job I want. The only thing I hate about these Saturday mornings is getting up so early. But if I was home, I'd probably have to clean the house, so I'd rather be here. It really gets my weekend going, and I know I'm needed here and it feels good."

When the half-hour is up, the girls return to the volunteer office. Just as they step inside, they hear the familiar *Rrrrring...* and they know they're once again needed somewhere in the hospital.

Chapter Three

Substance Abuse Prevention

The statistics are staggering. According to the Center for Substance Abuse Prevention, about 50 percent of 15-year-olds report having used drugs, while 57 percent of high school seniors have used alcohol within the past month. Researchers report that half of all car crashes (the number one killer of teens today) are alcohol- or drug-related. That's a lot of at-risk kids! Fortunately, teen volunteers can help reduce these tragic statistics.

Why volunteer?

Teens who work in the area of substance abuse prevention have many reasons for volunteering in the field. Specifically, some teens have said:

- *"It seems stupid to watch people risk their lives taking drugs and alcohol when they don't even know there are other ways to have fun. I want to give kids alternatives."*
- *"My best friend's little brother died while driving drunk. I saw what it did to his family, and I never want that to happen to mine."*
- *"My parents worry enough about me when I go out on the weekend. At least now they know I'm concerned about drinking, driving and drugs."*
- *"I volunteer in an emergency room, so I've seen all kinds of overdoses and DWI accidents. People learn about it in school, but I guess they just don't think anything will happen to them."*
- *"When I was a freshman, I used to get into the car with drunk juniors and seniors. I was always scared, but I wanted to be accepted. After we got into an accident one night, I decided to start a club for underclassmen so no one else would have to risk their life to fit in somewhere."*

Who can volunteer?

Boys and girls from their early to late teens fall victim to substance abuse, so boys and girls of all ages are needed in the field of substance abuse prevention. In school-based programs, everyone is welcome to join. There are also several substance abuse prevention organizations (like those listed in the Directory starting on page 127) that have specific eligibility requirements. But in general, most student organizations only require you to make a pledge of sobriety to become a member/volunteer.

Am I the right person?

Although all teens are welcome, some seem to be more effective in this field than others. The most successful volunteers usually have these characteristics:

- They have a personal interest in preventing teen substance abuse.
- They are committed and eager to see a change in their peer community.
- They work well with others.
- They learn from mistakes and are not judgmental of the people around them.
- They do not take it personally when other teens choose to ignore their advice and continue to use/abuse drugs and alcohol.
- They are patient and understanding.

Jeff Colford, now a 19-year-old college student, volunteered for Saferides, a local sober drivers program, during his junior and senior years in high school. Through Saferides, he offered rides home to students who had been drinking or using drugs. He believes that he needed all of the personality traits listed above at some point in his volunteering experience and adds: "Sometimes you get really frustrated because you see the same people getting high every weekend and needing a ride home. You just have to remember that some people can't control their problem. Alcoholism is a disease, and high school kids can have it just like anyone else."

Some things are private

Like volunteers in the health-care industry, volunteers in the field of substance abuse prevention must respect a person's right to privacy. If you volunteer in a hospital, clinic or rehabilitation center, what you learn about patients must not be discussed outside of the facility.

Or, if another teen confides in you about a drug or alcohol problem, you must not break that trust by talking about it to your friends. Substance abuse prevention volunteers must respect the privacy rights of others.

Driving under the influence of drugs or alcohol

According to researchers from Mothers Against Drunk Driving (MADD), in 1991, almost 3,000 people ages 16 to 20 died in alcohol- or drug-related car crashes. There are countless programs looking for volunteers with the dedication to reduce this figure in the future. A few notable programs are described here, but be sure to ask your guidance counselor about other local programs.

Sober drivers. Ask your guidance counselor or health teacher if your community has a sober drivers program in place on weekends and during vacation time. Volunteers in these programs offer a free and confidential ride home to students who have been drinking or using drugs. Volunteers are generally needed for two jobs:

1. When teens call the sober drivers hotline to ask for a ride, volunteers keep a written record of their current location and the location of their home. Drivers should not be used as a taxi service moving teens from party to party. The phone operator must make it clear that the caller is to be given transportation home only.
2. Volunteer drivers take teens under the influence of drugs or alcohol back to their homes. To do this, they need a valid driver's license and a vehicle to use during the evening.

Each community creates its own safety rules for the drivers. The most common rules are: all drivers work with a partner of the opposite sex; all cars must have a cellular phone or two-way radio; and no driver may transport more than two passengers at a time.

Students Against Driving Drunk (SADD). SADD has programs for kids at all age levels that raise awareness about the issue of drinking and driving. Just before the winter holidays, one SADD chapter put a wrecked car (donated by a local car-towing company) on the front lawn of the school. Next to it they put a huge red, black and green sign saying, "This Is the Danger of Driving Drunk." SADD chapter president Veronica Beach says, "If it saves one life or prevents one person from getting into a car and driving drunk, then it's worth it."

Each of the 17,000 SADD chapters around the country organize activities that they hope will keep their friends from drinking and driving. Some ring bells once every 23 minutes to highlight the fact that someone is killed in a drunken-driving accident every 23 minutes. Others form paper chains symbolizing a link that will not be broken by alcohol, while some groups perform mock accidents to bring the horror of real car accidents closer. Most raise money to buy and give away SADD key chains, designated driver ribbons and other novelties.

If you are interested in starting a SADD chapter in your school, contact SADD national headquarters (listed in the Directory) and ask for their booklet "How to Start Your SADD Chapter and New Ideas for Existing SADD Chapters."

Mothers Against Drunk Drivers (MADD). MADD's mission is to stop drunk drivers and to support their victims. Some of MADD's programs include: educating teens about prevention of car accidents; petitioning local, state and federal officials on enforcement of drunk driving laws; victim compensation; victim's rights and challenging the alcoholic beverage industry to market their products more conscientiously. MADD also uses teens to help distribute their "Contract for Life." This is an agreement between parents and kids. The teen agrees to call home for a ride if he or she is ever in a situation where the person driving is intoxicated. The parents agree to pick the teen up at any time without any discussing the incident until the following day. There is a similar pledge for student athletes.

As a grass roots organization, volunteers are the heart of MADD, and teenagers are welcome in many programs. For more information, call the MADD headquarters number listed in the Directory.

Remove Intoxicated Drivers (RID). There are RID chapters in 40 states; all are completely staffed by volunteers. RID chapters work with criminal justice agencies and other local groups to bring an end to drunk driving. They sponsor efforts in victim support, court monitoring, publicity and legislative policy-making. Teen volunteers are especially needed for office and clerical work. Call RID headquarters, listed in the Directory, to find the chapter nearest you.

Do it yourself

If your school or community doesn't have an organized program in place to deal with safe driving, you can get some action going yourself. Try these for starters:

- Organize a workshop on responsible driving. Contact CARS—Community for Automobile Responsibility and Safety, c/o David Street, 1222 N. Main St., Suite 815, San Antonio, TX 78212.
- Pass out buttons and bumper stickers. One popular sticker says, "Friends Don't Let Friends Drive Drunk." You can get these from Operation Cork, 8939 Via La Jolla, Suite 203, San Diego, CA 92037.
- Get more information about the need for driver safety by contacting the National Highway Traffic Safety Administration, Office of Traffic Safety Programs, NTS-01, Room 5125, 400 7th St. S.W., Washington, DC 20590.
- Ask permission to paint "Buckle-Up" symbols with traffic paint by the exits of your school parking lot.

Substance abuse prevention

According to the Center for Substance Abuse Prevention, 32 percent of high school seniors have taken five or more drinks in a row at least once within the previous two weeks; 27 percent have used marijuana in the past year, and 10 percent have used cocaine at least once. If these figures alarm you, you can change them by joining or starting a substance abuse prevention program.

Just Say No is a popular student volunteer program. This organization helps teens begin Just Say No drug-free programs in schools and communities. Their goal is to prevent drug abuse.

Teen members plan activities that educate students about the dangers of drugs, and they help create community interest and involvement in drug-free activities.

One Just Say No group wrote scripts and acted out scenes showing kids in different situations saying "no" to drugs. The scenes were videotaped and presented at a school drug awareness assembly. Joe DiGeronimo, one of the actors, wasn't sure he wanted to participate at first because the meetings were held during lunch period. But after the first meeting he was glad he joined: "It was really a lot of fun acting out the ways kids try to pressure other kids to use drugs. And it was good to practice all the different ways to say 'no.' "

You can find out about existing Just Say No programs in your area or get information to start your own group by calling the headquarters listed in the Directory.

Peer counseling

One way to lessen the frequency of chemical abuse among teens is to help them deal with the stresses that make drinking and drugs seem appealing. The transition into high school can be hard for students. Even for older teens, the academic demands of high school and the pressure to get into a good college can seem overwhelming. Peer counselors can help lessen the stress and keep kids from looking to alcohol and drugs for answers.

Teens are often the best people to help other teens. In some instances, they can offer an understanding and sympathetic ear that their peers may not find at home. They may also be able to undo the influence of negative peer pressure. Many teens will do whatever their friends do, even when they know it's wrong. Peer counselors can offer other teens a new way of looking at things, reasons to resist their friends and cause to trust their own good judgment.

If your school already has a peer counseling program, your first step will be training. If not, there are state, national and international organizations that can help your school develop a program. Just Say No International, for example, has a Youth Power training program for student leaders and adult advisors.

It's usually best not to counsel your friends about drugs or alcohol abuse without proper training. You may come into contact with people who have serious physical, emotional or psychological problems that you're not qualified to deal with. If you're not able to get training, the next best thing is to find out where there are professionals who can help. Talk to your guidance counselor and use the Directory to find sources of information.

Pulling it all together

Once you've joined or founded a program for substance abuse prevention, you'll be ready to do something that will make a difference. First, you and the other members will make a commitment to stay sober. Then you can organize fun activities for your classmates that do not involve drug or alcohol consumption.

The ideas are limitless—some groups have had picnics, dances, hay rides and in-line skating competitions. Members of SADD have been known to encourage parents to agree to provide supervised parties. They plan and publicize a blowout event for graduation where seniors can have fun and celebrate without chemicals. They also invite local celebrities and youth workers to address classes or assemblies. And most importantly, they don't ever drink and drive. Their example as student leaders is the best volunteer effort of all.

Whatever activities your group sponsors, the primary goal is to provide teens with opportunities to feel useful and needed without chemical stimuli. A strong sense of belonging with peers and community takes away one of the most common reasons teens abuse substances—loneliness.

Most volunteer programs need money to stay afloat, so many groups organize fund raisers. The basic cost of a sober drivers program, for example, includes advertising, phone expenses and mileage reimbursement for drivers using their own cars. Sometimes local government, service or community organizations, high schools or private businesses will sponsor such efforts if you ask. Also, volunteers across the country find thousands of creative and fun ways to raise money themselves. Car washes, benefit dances, candy sales, door-to-door canvassing and many more fund-raising activities help teens to help other teens.

National organizations

There are literally hundreds of national organizations dedicated to substance abuse prevention, education and treatment that do not work through schools. Many of these use teen volunteers at the state and local level.

The type of volunteer work you do will vary depending on the goals of the particular organization; local chapters adjust their programs to meet the needs of the communities they serve. Let's look at the National Council on Alcoholism and Drug Dependence (NCADD) as an example.

The NCADD is based in New York City and has local chapters in more than 35 states. Their mission is to educate the public about the nature of addiction, prevention and treatment. At the local level, this goal is achieved in hundreds of different ways, depending upon the needs of each community. One chapter may focus on educating young children. Another may focus on teaching women about the effects of alcohol on a developing fetus. As a volunteer, your work will be tied to the needs of your community.

Common tasks. Most of the organizations in the field of substance abuse prevention have headquarters offices that are staffed by part-time volunteers. Teens are most frequently used to answer the phone. If you volunteer to do this, a supervisor will train you on the proper procedure for handling phone calls, teach you phone courtesy and provide you with basic information to answer the most common questions. You may also be asked to help with other basic office duties like mailing, filing and light typing.

What to wear. Most offices will expect you to dress neatly, though casually. Average school clothes are usually acceptable.

How often? Your time commitment is entirely up to the organization's needs. Some are delighted if you can offer one hour a week whenever you can fit it in your schedule; others need more time, and they need it on a regular basis. When you call to ask about volunteer opportunities, be sure to ask what kind of time commitment is expected.

Rewards and recognition

For school-based volunteer programs, there may be monthly, quarterly and/or yearly awards given to students who make the biggest impact on the community. In weekly meetings, organization leaders often praise the people who have been working hard and encourage those who are just getting started. Or there may be no recognition program at all. But quite often, hard work does get noticed. One student in New Jersey, for example, was given a wall plaque recognizing his role in organizing and volunteering in a Saferides program. Others have seen their names and photographs on the office wall as "Volunteer of the Month."

And many others receive something even better: the good feeling that goes along with volunteering to help other teens. Here's what a few had to say about the rewards of volunteering:

"I don't really remember ever receiving an actual award. I'm just very proud of the fact that I might have saved someone's life."

— Dave Tosques, 20

Dave volunteered for a sober driver program in his senior year of high school. He is currently a college student.

"I like the way people respect my friends and me for doing what we do. I think it gives people a lot better picture of teenagers when they see us being responsible."

—Lauren Handel, 18

Lauren helped to organize sober activities for young people in her town. She plans to work for a sober driver program at the college she will be attending.

"I moved to a new town in my sophomore year of high school. By getting involved in a substance abuse prevention program, I met more people faster than I would have on my own. Now I keep at it because it makes me feel good to be doing something good."

—Tim Stafford, 17

Tim and four other teens do mailings on weekends for a county substance abuse prevention office.

Getting started

If your school has programs similar to the ones in this chapter, all you need to do is attend a meeting to join. If you want to start a program, read Chapter Eight and then get going!

- For local and county programs, there are volunteer offices that can connect you with the type of work you would like to do.
- To join a national group, find an organization that sounds interesting in the Directory and give them a call.
- Your guidance counselor also may know of places that need teen volunteers, and your county volunteer office also can help you.
- If you're having trouble, get *The Citizen's Alcohol and Other Drug Prevention Directory: Resources for Getting Involved*. This book lists more than 3,000 local, state and federal substance abuse prevention-related agencies. You or your school librarian can get a copy through the National Clearinghouse for Alcohol and Drug Information (see Directory for address).

There's certainly no shortage of opportunities for teens who want to do something about the shocking statistics that indicate substance abuse is a major problem for today's kids. So if you're ready to promise sobriety, there's much you can do to encourage your friends to do the same and live longer.

Resisting peer pressure: Jessica and Melinda

"Okay, guys. We need people partying, more kids arriving, lots of excitement and at least one drunk. Who wants to play the part of the drunk?"

The teens laugh and playfully attempt to shove each other forward. Then Kevin reluctantly stands up. "I'll do it for this rehearsal," he says. "But let's get someone else for the real skit. I'm not comfortable doing this with my father's history."

"I know," says director Melinda Bell compassionately. "But remember, it's really acting. You're playing the part of this guy Rob."

With clipboard in hand, Melinda explains the skits. "These are kids' parties in a town where there's a lot of drinking going on. We have to make it look convincing without getting ridiculous."

The kids are all members of the community's newly formed TGIF (Together Getting Into Focus) alcohol awareness action plan. The community team is composed of teachers, administrators, clergy, police, guidance counselors, parents and kids. They have planned an evening of workshops for ninth-grade students and their parents that will help students develop refusal skills.

At an earlier meeting during the summer, Melinda and her co-director, Jessica Muzzio, sat on the floor of their advisor's living room and wrote out the lines. The skits, which would be performed by their fellow students and peer leaders, would show a party in progress where alcohol was being consumed by some teens. The girls created a simple scenario with fake names and typical teenage dialogue.

Soon they were in rehearsals. And now they stand before their audience. Melinda greets the students and their parents and offers a brief explanation of the purpose of the skits. She also adds a disclaimer so that no finger-pointing will be done when the skits are over. Next, she explains where crucial items are to be imagined—table over here, some chairs there, and the door. Then they're ready to go.

"I can't wait for you to meet this guy Rob," says Lisa to her friend Diane as they approach the house. "He's cute, he's nice, he's smart. He even promised to help me with my algebra homework this weekend."

"You have to show him to me as soon as we get there!"

The girls enter the house, greet a few friends and then Rob walks over, obviously drinking.

"Hey, Lisa! You look great tonight."

"Hi, Rob. You look nice, too."

"Where's your drink, Lisa?—Wait, I'll get you one."

"No thanks, Rob. I don't drink."

"What do you mean, you don't drink? Everyone drinks. Come on. Come with me."

"No. Really, Rob, my parents would kill me if I did. Besides, I just don't want to."

"Wow, you seem really uptight. Come on, let's go upstairs. I'll help you loosen up."

As Rob grabs Lisa's arm, her face changes. Then the moderator steps into the scene to address the audience.

"We're going to freeze the action here," the moderator says. "Why do you think Lisa looks so scared?"

As members of the audience offer suggestions, the moderator turns to the girl playing Lisa. "Lisa, is he right? Do you think Rob's had too much to drink?" 'Lisa' stays in character, as do the rest of the actors, while the audience asks questions and offers opinions.

"Where are you kids getting all this liquor?"

"What exactly is everyone drinking?"

"Is *everyone* drinking?"

"Do your parents know?"

"Do you think you have a problem?"

"What do you do if you want to go to a party and don't want to drink?"

"Is it easy to get alcohol in this town?"

"Don't you feel guilty lying to your parents?"

It's hard for the actors to stay in character. These questions are sometimes difficult to field; things heat up and some parents become more accusing. But the point of the discussion is not to draw conclusions or give solutions. It is to raise awareness, and it works.

After calming down the group, the teens are ready to begin Part II.

"Okay, everyone," begins Jessica. "This is the same party as before, only about one hour later. Christine and Leah are approaching from outside and talking about what they think will be going on." Before signaling for action, Jessica reminds the audience that the scene is fictional.

"I've been thinking about this party all week. I can't wait to see who's here."

"Me too! But I really want to be careful about drinking. I don't want to get caught up in that. See, I've got my own soda to drink."

"Right. I have mine too. I'm not drinking either. We'll stick together and kind of support each other. Okay?"

"Okay."

As the girls enter, one of the other kids comes over to tell Christine about Rob and Lisa. Another girl approaches Leah with a beer in her hand.

"Hi, Leah! How are you? I haven't seen you in a long time. How's everything going?"

"Hey, what's up?"

"We're all having a great time. What've you got there? Soda? Come with me; we can add something to that."

"No thanks. I promised Christine I wouldn't..."

"What is she, your baby sitter? Besides, where is she? She didn't even stick around."

The action continues, and Leah takes a drink just as Christine returns. The moderator again stops the action.

"Why do you think Christine looks startled?" she asks the audience.

As the freshmen and their parents respond, another round of questions and answers begins, this time focusing on peer pressure and peer responsibility. Sometimes the questions seem to come faster than the actors can respond, and the moderator is needed to keep things from getting out of hand. Parents show the tension they're feeling through body language—by folding their arms and legs, tapping their feet and sitting back in their chairs. The ninth graders, on the other hand, open up by leaning forward or by standing up.

Toward the end of the "in character" discussion about teenage drinking, the players ask if they can drop their roles. They want to talk to the audience as "real" kids, not as actors.

"It's true that there's a lot of drinking at teenage parties," they admit. "But there are ways to avoid it." They emphasize the need for peer support, and they offer ideas like bringing your own non-alcoholic drinks. They also caution the parents to stay in touch with their kids. "Ask your kids where they're going and who they're with!" say the actors firmly. "And check up on it!" says the girl who played to role of Lisa. "My parents are probably the sole reason I haven't had a drink at a party. They'd kill me!"

Jessica and Melinda meet again with the freshmen and their parents during a social hour after all the skits are completed.

"We didn't want to scare anyone, but we want people to know the truth," says Melinda. "We don't have the answers," adds Jessica. "We just want to make sure everyone knows what's going on and offer some suggestions about how teens can help."

Their ideas and suggestions were gratefully received by the students and their parents. One mother commented as she was leaving, "Those kids were so convincing, it was scary. I'm going to pay a lot more attention to my kids."

Chapter Four

The Needy

In every state, in every town, in every neighborhood, there are needy people. The needy are the homeless, the hungry, the illiterate, the poor. They are victims of earthquakes, hurricanes, tornadoes and floods. They are babies, they are teens, they are elderly. All of them need your help.

Why volunteer?

The needy are those who most directly benefit from volunteer efforts. Why you may choose to help them is personal, reflecting your own needs and beliefs, but on the next page you'll find what some teens had to say about their reasons for volunteering.

- *"At first I just wanted something to write on my college application, but I ended up wishing I had started sooner."*

- *"It feels good just to help somebody who needs your help."*
- *"Jesus said to love your neighbor as yourself. This is kind of religious, but as human beings it should be our nature to want to help the people around us—especially those who really need it."*
- *"People trust you when they find out you're a volunteer. I didn't know that at first, but now people want to approach me—they see me as a really friendly person."*
- *"I get depressed seeing how so many people are so much worse off than me. I do volunteer work only on Saturdays, but it makes me feel better to know that I'm trying to help."*

Am I cut out for this?

For whatever reason you decide to volunteer, certain personality traits make the experience more fulfilling. Teens who volunteer to help the needy often have these characteristics:

- They aren't judgmental toward those less fortunate than themselves.
- They are responsible and committed.
- They are compassionate and concerned for the welfare of others.
- They follow orders well.
- They can deal with meeting people who have not bathed, are poorly clothed or are suffering.
- They are team players.

Amanda Bell, a 17-year-old volunteer in a high school service club, adds one more personality trait that has been invaluable to her: the willingness to talk to strangers. "Once I served dinner at a shelter for the homeless," she remembers. "Not only did we eat with the people there, but we sat and talked to them, which was not a comfortable experience for me at first. It's really hard to talk to someone who is so stigmatized by society. But they really want to talk. So you just sit there and listen, and you realize that they're really interesting people. You just have to be able to talk to them and listen to them."

If you volunteer to help the needy, you must always remember that you are helping human beings. Many people you'll meet feel ashamed and alone. The volunteers who do the greatest good are those who can help others while allowing them to keep their dignity.

Requirements

In short, everyone is welcome and needed. Some jobs, such as helping to rebuild old and damaged buildings, require physical or skill commitments that you may not be able to meet. But there are so many ways to help the needy that there is something for everyone to do.

Many organizations have a minimum age requirement for volunteering, usually 13 years old for simple, safe tasks and 16 or 18 years old for potentially dangerous or highly skilled labor. If you are under legal age, you may need your parent or guardian's written permission to volunteer. The main requirement, though, is having the determination to make life a little better for as many people as you can.

Helping the homeless

Once upon a time, people used to think that homelessness was only a problem in big cities like New York, Houston or Los Angeles. But now we know that homelessness occurs in nearly every type of city, town and village.

There are several national organizations that deal directly with the housing needs of the homeless. Christmas in April USA and Habitat for Humanity International, for example, help the elderly, disabled and low-income population to find safe and inexpensive housing. A large part of their work is in the rebuilding and renovating of run-down buildings.

Some of these organizations require their laborers to be of legal age and to have experience in a related trade, such as carpentry or plumbing. Others allow young volunteers on construction sites as long as they are supervised and do not use power tools. In all cases, teen volunteers are frequently used in local offices to help with mailing, office work and fund raising. To find out if there is a branch office of a national organization near you, contact the headquarters listed in the Directory.

All 50 states have many shelters that provide temporary housing for the homeless. Teen volunteers in shelters are needed for a variety of jobs. They help with maintenance; there's always painting, cleaning and repairing to do. They may cook, serve and clean up daily meals. They do laundry, vacuum, dust, sew curtains and mend pillowcases and sheets. They receive new residents, play with children and sometimes—perhaps most important of all—volunteers just talk and listen.

In cities where the homeless have special needs, there are local organizations that address the specific needs of their communities. In New York City, for example, the Legal Action Center for the Homeless was formed to meet the legal needs of the homeless. Such organizations frequently use teen volunteers for clerical jobs, mail preparation and phone work. Your state office of volunteerism (listed in the Directory) will tell you where you can find these agencies that work behind the scenes to better the lives of the homeless.

Helping the poor

According to the U.S. Bureau of the Census, more than 15 percent of all families and 21 percent of all children live below the poverty line. This means that about 36 million people in our country are without enough money to afford the basics of food, shelter and clothing.

There are more organizations dedicated to fighting hunger and poverty than any other area of service. The prospects for teen volunteers are endless. If you live in a farming community, you may become involved with a member group of the Gleaning Network; these volunteers pick up the food that remains after farmers harvest their crops and distribute it to the poor. If you live in an urban area, organizations like USA Harvest collect donated food and distribute it to local soup kitchens and shelters. Or, for a local Salvation Army chapter, you may prepare and serve food for the needy or collect and distribute used clothing to Salvation Army thrift shops.

In addition to these large, ongoing national programs, there are food and clothing drives sponsored every day by local clubs, schools and churches. Whether you join an existing program or start your own, you can expect to do any one of these tasks:

- Contact local restaurants, merchants and hotels to ask for contributions of food, items for personal hygiene and used linens, pillows and beds.
- Stand by at a donation site where students and residents can drop off donated food and clothing.
- Package the donated goods and transport them to the kitchens, shelters and other places where they are needed.

Soup kitchens also rely heavily on teen volunteers. You may be asked to prepare or serve the food; in that case, you will have to follow the same sanitary requirements as a restaurant employee, which means washing your hands and tying back or netting your hair. Or, you may be most useful as a dish washer when the meal is completed.

If you worry about how you'll feel working with the poor, keep in mind the story of Jacob Moskowitz: "At first I felt so sorry for the people at the shelter that I was scared to even look them in they eye. My supervisor noticed that I looked uncomfortable, so he took me aside. He told me that I should think of them as guests stopping over for dinner. Guests should always feel welcome."

The illiterate

Those in poverty need food, shelter and clothing. But to break the cycle of poverty, they need to be able to read and their children need to learn the importance of reading. Millions of people cannot read; many don't even have access to books if they wanted to learn. Giving people the tools to read is as important as giving them the material things they lack. And here again, teens can help.

If your school or library already has a program in place—join it! If not—start one! There are lots of things teens can do to help. You can hold a book drive to collect books and then distribute them to shelters, thrift shops or after-school programs. You can start a story hour for young children on Saturday mornings. You can help tutor elementary school children after school. There's more specific information on tutoring in Chapter Five. Read it over and then think of ways to combine fighting illiteracy with helping the poor and needy.

Natural and man-made disasters

Every year, natural and man-made disasters force human beings around the world into the category of "needy." Natural disasters are those caused by floods, tornadoes, earthquakes, hurricanes and so on. Man-made disasters are those caused by things such as bombs and fire. Whatever the cause, whole communities are sometimes left in need of food, clothing and shelter. There are many organizations dedicated to helping these people when tragedies strike, and they could use your help.

Groups like CARE, Food for the Hungry and the American Red Cross collect and distribute food, clothing, medical supplies and equipment to disaster victims. Teen volunteers are particularly needed to collect the supplies, raise money and to help run regional offices. Many students have also been able to offer help right at the site of the disaster. This often happens when a school group raises money to transport students to the disaster area and provides for their needs while they offer volunteer assistance.

Volunteering for disaster relief can be a year-round effort. Because disasters occur without warning, the relief organizations must be prepared at all times. They can't wait for the disaster to strike and then look around for food and money. To do this they need continuous volunteer efforts to collect food, clothing, relief supplies and money. Call one of the organizations listed in the Directory and find out what you can do today.

School-based groups

There are many national and local organizations that welcome teens in their efforts to help the needy. But if you don't want to make a commitment right now to a large group, look around your school. Many schools have some kind of club dedicated to helping the needy. If your school does, why not join it? If it doesn't, why not start one?

You may find your volunteer efforts are more enjoyable when you work alongside kids your own age. There are more opportunities to show leadership and initiative in school-based programs. And very often, you can do more to meet the needs of people in your area when you put together your own organization.

If you want to start your own program to help the needy there are lots of groups that can assist you. You might contact the National Student Campaign Against Hunger and Homelessness. If you become an affiliate of this group, you will receive resources, advice and ideas that will help you and your friends make a positive impact on your community.

Summer camp

If your school activities don't give you enough time to participate in volunteer work, but you're still interested in helping the needy, a summer camp program may be just right for you.

Pearl Chao spent the summer between her junior and senior years volunteering at Camp Lots of Fun—a two-week day camp for homeless children ages 5 to 12. As a volunteer counselor, Pearl was responsible for supervising a small group of children each day. She would prepare their breakfast, take them to the park for nature hikes and play games like tag or Monopoly. Pearl also watched them during swim time, organized sports activities like baseball and kickball games and accompanied them on field trips.

Besides the valuable lessons she learned about the everyday needs of the homeless, Pearl also learned something about herself. "Most people don't live as well as I do," she says. "I used to take things for granted, but not anymore."

If volunteering at a summer camp sounds like a good idea to you, call the National Coalition for the Homeless (see Directory) and ask if there's a summer camp for homeless children in your area. They're sure to need your help.

Getting started

If you want to volunteer to help the needy, there are many ways to begin.

- Your church or synagogue should be able to point you in the right direction. They may even sponsor programs of their own that need teen volunteers.
- Your guidance counselor can tell you about the school- and community-based organizations in your town.
- The county or state volunteer agency (listed in the Directory) can connect you with groups that are recruiting teen volunteers.
- You can contact national organizations directly. Call their headquarters number listed in the Directory to find a local branch.

Recognition and rewards

The recognition and rewards given to those who volunteer to help the needy are as many and as varied as the assistance programs. Some groups, like the Salvation Army, have an established system of service recognition for certain volunteer efforts. Others give certificates of appreciation, letters of thanks, service pins or just a simple "thank you" and a handshake.

Regardless of the reward system, you can be sure that any time and effort you contribute will be noticed and appreciated by those whose opinion matters most: the needy. That's why most volunteers find that service awards are not the most treasured aspect of volunteering. Like these teens, they find they get back more than they give:

"The satisfaction of helping somebody, of seeing them happy, is the reward I get."
—Mike Trinh, 16
Mike is a member of a high school group that regularly volunteers at a community food bank; they reprocess slightly damaged food that cannot be sold in supermarkets. The repackaged food is then distributed to the hungry.

"You meet interesting people doing this, and they aren't always the volunteers. You learn a lot, too."
—Amanda Bell, 17
Amanda has volunteered at a homeless shelter.

"When I can do something for someone that they cannot do for themselves, it makes me feel happy. It makes me feel good about myself."

—Anay Patel, 17

Anay belongs to a school club that is dedicated to helping those less fortunate.

"You shouldn't volunteer just because it's good 'application ink.' When people say that, it gets me mad. I get so much more out of volunteering than that."

—Angela Fortunato, 17

Through her high school service club, Angela has volunteered in several projects for the homeless and the needy.

"I always wanted to get involved in clubs and things, but I don't really have any special talents. Now I know I'm good at helping people, and I'm involved in something good."

—James Chaplin, 17

Jim is the president of his high school community service club, called Project Interact. He has helped in book drives, food distribution and general service to his community.

As you can tell from the experiences of these teens, whatever you do for the needy is returned to you in feelings of pride and accomplishment. Take a look at the story about Mike Forshay and you'll see what I mean.

The rewards of helping those in need: Mike Forshay

"During the summer of 1993, rain pounded the Midwest for weeks on end. The TV brought the reality of the unrelenting flood waters right into my East Coast living room. I remember seeing whole city streets drowned beneath raging flood waters. On every channel I saw replays of entire homes being swept away by the current, and I saw the numbed faces of the people who were the victims of nature's wrath. These people needed help—but at age 16, what could I do?

"The answer to that question came from my dad, who is a deacon at our church. One morning he asked me to help him think of ways we could ease the burden of these people. We agreed that we could raise money to help them put their lives back together. This sounded like a good way to do *something*. But that wasn't the end of my dad's plan. He asked me if, after we collected the money, I'd like to go with him to deliver it and find out what else we could do in person. I have to admit that this wasn't exactly how I had planned to spend my summer vacation. But it did sound adventurous, and I couldn't forget the faces of those people I had seen on TV—so I agreed.

"The first thing we had to do was to organize fund raisers. We contacted local churches, explained our plans and asked for donations from the congregations. In two weeks, we had collected $8,000. Then before I knew it, my dad and I were on a plane headed for Des Moines, Iowa.

"When we arrived at the airport, we were warmly greeted by four of our soon-to-be friends from a nearby Catholic parish. They brought us to Visitation Church where we would stay in the rectory guest room on cots.

"During the ride to the church, we heard more about the destruction caused by the flood. We learned that the tap water was no longer running because the sewers had leaked into the water supply contaminating it. Many businesses, restaurants and stores were shut down. And many roads were closed, making travel very difficult. We got to bed early that night not knowing what we were in for the next day.

"The first morning, my dad and I were asked if we'd help some parishioners whose houses had been flooded. We rented a car and we set off to a section of town about a mile away. When we arrived, we looked around to find that the damage didn't seem as bad as it did on television—but still there was work to do. We spent the morning cleaning out sewage-filled basements of impoverished people. The work was dirty, exhausting and certainly needed to be done, but still we wondered where was the destruction we had seen on television.

"After finishing the job and eating lunch offered from a Salvation Army truck, we asked about the devastated areas we had heard about. We were given directions across town to the river. We headed off, not really knowing who or what we'd find.

"Each block closer to the river brought us into the thick of the flood's destruction. We were taken aback by the ruined houses, the deserted cars filled with water, the garages ripped right out of the ground. I had never imagined that water could cause so much damage. We went right to work, helping in the preliminary stages of rebuilding three houses on the bank of the river.

"For the next few days, we cleared out the garbage, mud, sewage and destroyed furniture from these houses. We worked alongside a group of people who had driven down from Canada to help. It was rewarding to see the unconditional love of people for others. Here we were, not knowing who we were helping, but rebuilding their houses and trying to make their lives normal again. Working from about 9:00 in the morning to 4:30 in the afternoon each day, my dad and I, along with our new group of friends, helped make these homes livable again.

"After doing everything we could do in those houses, we moved on. We searched the damaged areas for workers who needed help. There were so many people in need, it was difficult to pick and choose which ones to assist. Soon we found two men who were working hard to repair their business, which had been wiped out. We spent half a day cleaning the building inside and out. We painted the walls and left the building sparkling white, which really stood out against the mud-encrusted background of the buildings around it!

"There were many families who had been working hard but getting nowhere until work crews like my dad and I came in from around the country. It was wonderful to help people who were in such need and who were so appreciative. One couple I remember in particular was Paul and Irene Galvin. They were an older couple who really had no way of repairing their house. Irene was so crippled by arthritis that she couldn't get to the basement where all the damage was. And Paul, a veteran with no legs, was bound to his wheelchair. My father and I worked all day draining water and cleaning their basement. The Galvins couldn't thank us enough. During our break, Irene made and served us lunch despite her arthritis. When Paul, the tough-as-nails veteran, broke down in tears, I couldn't help but think how blessed I am. To see this family in such need made me stop and think about all the things I take for granted. Here I was running up and down stairs all day without giving it a thought, and the Galvins couldn't get down the stairs even once to save their home.

"Another instance that really touched me was the case of a woman named Opal Wickett. Opal was as 73-year-old widow whose small house was destroyed by the savage flood. When we met her, Opal was living in a friend's small motor home with no idea how she was going to survive. I felt sort of guilty about all the silly things I had worried about in the past, when here was a desperate, distraught widow who didn't have a house or flood insurance and couldn't pay to have it repaired. Still she was determined to get back on her feet.

"We could do nothing for Opal's house because rebuilding was beyond our capabilities. But we felt we had to do something. So we decided, as did many others, to give her a donation. We gave Opal $500 of the money we had collected from the generous people back home. This would be enough to buy her a new water heater. Opal's thanks was overwhelming. I felt as though I had saved her life. She didn't have anything to give us in return, so she gave us her tears.

"The thanks we received from everyone we helped was from the heart. Even children who had been living in trailers for a month were grateful, returning our gift of a few hundred dollars with hugs and kisses. And you know what? It was worth every cent. The most memorable part of the trip wasn't the publicity in the newspapers, and it wasn't the thanks given to us for our small part in helping others. It was the love I felt during the time I spent there. When people, who don't even know each other, work to repair the house of a total stranger, there is an almost visible feeling of love and caring. People driving along the road would get out and begin to help. Others, like us, traveled from far and wide to help the people of this town without expectations of rewards.

"Yet the rewards of my service to the people of this community are never ending. The warmth they showed me made me feel like I was on top of the world. The love I gave to them was returned tenfold. After the trip, my dad and I received so much mail from everybody—our co-workers, the victims of the flood, the members of the church where we stayed—everybody. We've kept in close touch with the families we helped. We received a newspaper article that featured Opal Wickett as she moved back into her house once again. I felt like I, in a small way, helped Opal rebuild her life. Even today, we hear from some of the families as they tell us of their successes and accomplishments. I still feel great joy every time I hear from somebody in Des Moines.

"The work I did for one week has really changed my life. It made me think about all the things I'm blessed with. I no longer take simple things for granted. The love and sharing has stayed with me over these years. Although I asked for nothing in return, I was given so much."

Chapter Five

Education

Volunteerism in the field of education is very popular because there are so many ways and so many places you can do it. The thousands of elementary schools, adult schools, religious schools, tutoring programs and nursing homes that dot the United States need qualified, willing volunteers like you.

Why should I volunteer?

Teens have many reasons for donating their time and energy to helping others in the field of education. Some have said:

- *"I just enjoy helping others."*
- *"I think I want to teach, and I need some experience."*

- *"A friend of mine really liked doing it, so I thought I'd give it a try."*
- *"I think it's important for children who are underprivileged and whose parents can't afford tutoring to receive help."*
- *"My scout troop volunteered in a local school; I just stuck with it after the program was over."*
- *"My mom thought it would be a good experience for me—and she was right!"*
- *"I saw a TV show that showed volunteers teaching and it looked like fun."*
- *"My temple recently welcomed back members who returned from a trip across the United States teaching adult literacy. I decided I wanted to get involved, too."*

Do I have to?

When you volunteer to tutor, you make a commitment to the people who count on your help. For example, picture that your church has a bilingual education class scheduled. The teacher expects an overflow crowd and asks you to help out. But come the day of the class, you decide to go mountain biking with your friends. While your church knows that it must be flexible when scheduling volunteers, it also expects you to show up when you say you will. Reliability is a big asset in the volunteer.

There's another reason you'll want to make sure you keep your commitment to tutor. A bond grows between a tutor and student during the course of a class or semester. This attachment is quite natural and can be one of the most rewarding aspects of your volunteer experience. Because tutoring programs usually require one-on-one attention, you'll disappoint your student if you don't show up.

Who is qualified?

While most of you are qualified to tutor, you will not be a teacher in the traditional school sense. Elementary and high school teachers need to be certified with a college degree. Your role as teacher will be to provide some extra help. As a middle or high school student, you're fully prepared to tutor younger children. You already know the basics they need to learn. Remember, these children are missing the fundamentals of education that you take for granted. You may not have a teacher's certificate, but if you are able to read this book, you are qualified to volunteer to help another student.

Who needs you?

There are innumerable places where volunteer teachers are needed. Take a look at these general categories that commonly use teen volunteers.

The functionally illiterate. Imagine that you never learned the basics in elementary school. Would it be possible to move on to more advanced education or get a driver's license if you could not read or write? Imagine being unable to read a menu, job application or bus schedule. If a person carries on a seemingly normal life, but cannot read these things, that person is considered functionally illiterate.

Consider these numbers:

- People who are functionally illiterate have reading skills at the fourth grade level.
- The National Commission on Excellence in Education reports that 13 percent of all 17-year-olds in the United States are functionally illiterate.
- Among minority youth, functional illiteracy now approaches 40 percent.
- The United States ranks 49th among 156 United Nations member countries in its rate of literacy, a drop of 18 places since 1950.
- 700,000 teens graduate each year unable to read their diplomas.
- Fewer than 5 percent of 17-year-olds in American schools read well enough to understand average college-level or business writing.

The common factor shared by almost all of the functionally illiterate in this country is that somewhere during their early school years they were cut off from learning. This can happen for lots of reasons. Maybe there was a lack of interest, lack of attention or resources, or maybe the parents weren't able or available to be supportive. Whatever the reason, there are many people in this country who cannot read. That's where you come in. As a literate teenager, you already have a reading level that is at least two to four times higher than a youngster in elementary school. You can teach the basics of reading to these kids who need you.

Inner-city children

Many inner-city children live with obstacles that often get in the way of learning how to read. Many of these kids live at or near the poverty line, forcing them to think more about their next meal than about their school work. Combine this with problems like crime and drugs, and you have prime candidates for functional illiteracy.

Fortunately, there are many programs that are in place to help these children. YMCAs, hospitals, shelters, libraries, schools and national and regional organizations (like those listed in the Directory under Education) all have volunteer programs to fight inner-city illiteracy. And they all need more help.

Many organizations run programs that use teen volunteers for lots of activities. You might be needed to:

- Read stories on Saturday mornings to groups of young children.
- Collect used books to distribute to shelters and day-care centers.
- Organize a fund raiser to buy school supplies, puzzles and "fun" books.
- Be a homework helper in an after-school program.

If you are feeling ambitious, you might even start your own group of teen volunteers for education. Many organizations like the Key Club and the Reading is Fundamental group will give you materials and guidance to start your own tutoring program. Or you can use your own creativity to create any number of programs like local story hours, flash card programs, homework clubs or reading marathons. Be sure to read Chapter Eight for the details on starting your own volunteer group. It can be lots of fun, but there are some basics you need to know before you begin.

Your friends

In your own school, you might enjoy peer tutoring. There are plenty of kids all around you who need extra help in many subjects from algebra to woodworking. In-school tutoring programs can be run before or after school, during lunch periods or even at the library in the evening.

Seventeen-year-old Alicia Cox tutors algebra during her lunch period for 20 minutes every day. "Usually I just help this boy by going over his homework and explaining the class lesson," says Alicia. "I think he's embarrassed to ask questions in class and then he gets lost. But with me, he feels more relaxed and we can straighten out his problems before they get too big."

Alicia began tutoring when her teacher asked her to help her classmate. In other schools, tutoring activities are often sponsored by the National Honor Society or the Student Council. If your school has this kind of program—why not join it? If it doesn't—read Chapter Eight and find out how you can start one!

Teens with troubles

Peer counseling or peer mediation is another way friends help friends in school. This is similar to peer tutoring, but it usually deals with situations outside the classroom that influence how well the student can concentrate on school work. Peer counselors are volunteers trained by guidance counselors and other special personnel to help people their own age deal with a variety of problems. While they can't always solve the classmate's problem, these student counselors provide a sympathetic ear.

The problems they deal with might include a fight between a boyfriend and a girlfriend, trouble with a certain class or teacher or peer pressure. "Everything is confidential, so nothing will be repeated," says 16-year-old Dana Devereaux, a high school junior who volunteers as a conflict manager. "Kids feel more comfortable talking about their problems because there are no teachers involved."

But the problems may also include more serious issues like drug abuse, dysfunctional families or unwanted pregnancies.

In these cases, the student counselors are trained to alert the school guidance department or psychologist. "If they say anything about suicide or abuse," says 17-year-old Blythe Boydston, another trained conflict manager, "we listen to their problems, but then we try to convince them to talk to a teacher or counselor."

If you volunteer to be any kind of peer counselor, you have to know how to keep a secret. All discussions and advice are confidential to protect the students' right to privacy.

Many schools across the country have adopted peer counseling programs to deal with the growing number of teen-related problems. These programs rely on teen volunteers who work within the educational system to help other teens work through their personal problems.

Younger kids

You might feel most comfortable tutoring younger kids in your own school district. Lots of schools set up programs that let the junior and high school students tutor the elementary school students. Members of the Future Educators of America, for example, not only help out in the classroom as teacher's aides, but they also set up after-school tutoring sessions to work with kids who want extra help.

In a program called VISTE (Volunteers in Service to Education) teens volunteer to tutor one student from September through June. Seventeen-year-old Clara Kuhlman has been volunteering with VISTE for three years now. She meets with her assigned fourth-grade student in the school library for a half-hour session once a week. Clara gets a textbook and encouragement from the classroom teacher, and she gets a sense of accomplishment for herself. "I started because I thought I wanted to be a teacher," she says. "Now I can't really say what I get out of it, but by the end of the year, I know my student looks forward to our meetings, and that makes me feel good."

Check the Directory in the back of the book to get more information about the Future Educators of America club.

Your church or synagogue

Religious institutions have a close relationship with education. Many of the early elementary schools, colleges and universities were run by religious groups. In today's society, religious organizations take a smaller role in education because public education is fully funded by the government, but religious education is still an integral part of any religion or denomination. Bible school, Sunday school or Hebrew school are just some examples of religious instruction where volunteers are needed. Religious groups need volunteers to staff these programs, as well as their day camps, summer camps, day-care centers and after-school programs.

Sixteen-year-olds Danielle Bertollo and Melissa Londregan co-teach a third-grade Sunday school class. Danielle began volunteering a year ago in order to meet the service requirements of her Confirmation class. This year she's continuing because she enjoys it. Melissa saw a plea from the church in the weekly bulletin and decided to give it a try.

Teaching from a textbook, Danielle and Melissa prepare each weekly lesson, organize class art projects and spend lots of time just talking to their students. While hoping this experience will help her meet her goal of becoming an elementary school teacher, Danielle also has other objectives. "I feel really good about myself," she says, "knowing that I'm doing something to help these kids get closer to God." Melissa adds that it has advantages for the students too. "I think it's important for the kids to have people our age to talk to—not just adults all the time," she says. "We can relate to them."

Fifteen-year-old Alycia Buraus is a classroom aide every Sunday morning in her parish's third-grade CCD program. Alycia helps the teacher by taking attendance, handing out supplies, correcting homework, reading stories, running errands and doing whatever else is helpful. "I enjoy working with kids," says Alycia.

"When I get more experience and feel more comfortable controlling the kids, I think I'll ask for my own class. It's a real good feeling knowing that I'm needed and feeling like I've helped my church."

Contact your church or synagogue to find out how you can help.

Adults

Do you know an adult in need of tutoring? Chances are there are more than a few right in your neighborhood. Look at these numbers:

- A Department of Education study on adult performance levels discovered that more than one in five adults are unable to perform ordinary reading tasks such as ordering a meal from a menu or filling out a job application.
- The National Assessment of Educational Progress recently reported on the literacy skills of America's young adults (21 to 25 years of age). They found that 80 percent couldn't read a bus schedule, 73 percent couldn't interpret a newspaper story and 63 percent couldn't follow written map directions.
- 43 percent of those seeking unemployment insurance have literacy deficiencies.

If you can read, you have valuable knowledge that you can share with the many adults who are looking for help. At first you may feel awkward "teaching" someone who may be as old as your parents. At the same time, that person may feel embarrassed to be learning from someone as young as you. That's why a smile and a positive attitude are your most important tools when tutoring adults.

Many adult literacy programs are organized by libraries and adult community schools. Although you're not qualified to teach these courses, you can be a classroom aide or you might offer to give a student extra help after class. You might just listen to a student read and help with difficult words. You might help homework assignments. Or you might simply explain how to read a bus schedule or read a newspaper.

If you think you'd like to work with adults, ask your local or school librarian to help you find a literacy program in your area. You can also call Literacy Volunteers of America (see Directory) for a referral to the adult literacy program closest to your home.

Immigrants—young and old

After immigrating to the United States, a number of foreign-speaking people live in city sections or towns where they can share their language and customs with fellow immigrants. For recent immigrants, it is very comforting to speak the native tongue.

Although these people are literate in their own languages, they need help understanding and learning English. As an English-speaking person, your vocabulary and grammar skills are invaluable to immigrants. If you happen to be of the same ethnic background or know their native tongue, your services are especially needed.

Of course, you are not certified to actually teach English as a second language. But as in any literacy program, you can help in simple, but meaningful, ways. You can offer to give extra help to students enrolled in classes. You can offer to read the newspaper to immigrants who need to hear the sound of our language. You can patiently listen as students attempt to read. You can simply be available to talk—talking is the best way to learn a new language.

Look around—where are there groups of recent immigrants who need tutoring? They may be in your school, in your religious organization, in a neighboring town. Act like a detective: Ask your guidance counselor, your minister, priest or rabbi, your town librarian. Tutoring new immigrants is a very special way to say, "Welcome to America."

Anywhere else?

Teaching doesn't happen in classrooms alone. Do you have a special skill or talent? Do you play basketball or baseball? Do you sew or knit? Do you play an instrument? Whatever your talent, you can volunteer to teach it to others. All around you there are after-school programs, YMCAs, Boys and Girls Clubs, day-care centers, camps, sport leagues and other organizations that would love to have you share your skills with their children.

Think about it. If you have the time and the desire, there's a group somewhere in your area that would benefit from your willingness to teach what you know.

Look like a teacher

When you volunteer for an organization you become the symbol of the organization you represent. So, the behavior and personality you show are very important. Here are some guidelines you might be asked to follow if you volunteer to work with an organization:

- Do not eat or drink while you are tutoring or are in front of a class.
- Do not chew gum loudly or blow bubbles.
- Avoid behavior that might intimidate or offend your students. Small children look up to you and might be hurt by your criticism. Older students might be offended if you are overly critical.
- Be respectful.
- Be sensitive to the fact that it may be difficult for some to seek help.
- Be cheerful and positive.

Along with some simple behavior guidelines like these, you may be asked to adhere to a general dress code. No one will make you wear a uniform, but your clothing should help you appear professional. Here are some suggestions:

- Don't wear ripped or torn jeans.
- Avoid certain T-shirts like those with messages that might be inappropriate or offensive.
- Stay away from jewelry, body art or clothing that may be viewed negatively by some students and may even scare younger children.

A bad match

It takes a special kind of person to volunteer successfully in education. So this field of service isn't for everyone. Listen to what one girl had to say about making the wrong volunteer choice:

> *"This girl I volunteered with would never stay the amount of time she was supposed to. We usually worked in pairs at the day-care center, and several times we worked together. It was always one excuse or another why she should leave early. Finally I confronted her, and she told me she was doing this for her resume and didn't really like the idea of wasting her time with little children. I didn't know how to answer, but it helped me realize that you shouldn't work with little kids unless you really want to."*

A bad match isn't unusual, and it's not something to get down about. As you know, education isn't the only field where volunteers are needed. And sometimes, the problem isn't really with education itself at all, but the area of education you've chosen. In the previous situation, the girl's partner may have felt more comfortable volunteering to help people her own age or older. If you think you are in a "bad match" situation, consider the following:

- *"My friend asked me to volunteer with her at the nursing home teaching stroke victims basic reading and speech skills. I was excited about volunteering but couldn't handle the nursing home atmosphere. After three weeks, I told my friend that I couldn't volunteer anymore. I felt really guilty about quitting until I joined a group in my church that helps inner-city kids with their reading. That was two years ago, and I've been helping them ever since."*
- *"My first experience helping others is one I'll never forget. The staff at the literacy center seemed unconcerned about my schedule. I was asked to come in for three hours and wound up staying six or seven hours every weekend for a month. I didn't mind helping, but it was starting to affect my school work. I tried to explain, but when they didn't get the message, I quit. Two months later I realized I missed*

volunteering, so I got in touch with my local library and now I'm back volunteering on a better schedule."

- *"I grew up in a Spanish-speaking household. When it came time to volunteer for high school credit, I thought it would be perfect to tutor my friends in Spanish. I would be helping them, strengthening my Spanish and getting credit—what a mistake. Just about every student knew me, and we got very little work done because we would spend the time socializing. After about a month, I switched from helping my classmates to helping adults at the community center. At least now I'm getting some work done."*

What do you get out of it?

The opportunities for volunteering in education are vast. So sometimes it takes a while to find just the right place. But when you do, you'll soon see that along with your students, you, too, benefit from the experience. Very practical benefits include:

- **Learning more about the subject you tutor**. Teaching others improves your own skills whether you tutor math, English, piano or swimming.
- **Resume building**. The hours you spend volunteering will enhance your resume, especially if you want to get a degree in teaching.
- **Learning patience and compassion**. Teaching is a one-on-one experience that lets you really get to know the people you help and teaches you how to take things in very small steps.

In addition to these very practical benefits, most volunteers just plain feel good about themselves when they give others the gift of knowledge. This good feeling is a great boost to your self-esteem and encourages you to go for goals you may never have attempted to reach before. You see, volunteering isn't all about helping others, it's about helping yourself as well.

The joy of teaching: John Romanick

Hidden among a row of industrial buildings, just behind the railroad tracks that cut through this small, suburban town, is a gymnasium where young gymnasts prepare for future competitions. Once inside, you realize that the atmosphere is similar to any other sporting event involving youngsters. Parents watch their children and chat with the parents of other young athletes. Stories are exchanged, coffee is sipped and, as always, the perpetual fund raiser is underway. The routine is broken only by a round of applause or an occasional yell of encouragement. On this late autumn night, however, a group of special gymnasts are in the middle of their weekly session which will prepare them for an event held every June—the Special Olympics.

The Special Olympics provide year-round sports training and athletic competition in a variety of Olympic-type sports for children and adults with mental retardation. This gives them opportunities to develop physical fitness, demonstrate courage, experience joy and participate in the sharing of skills and friendships. The people who train these special athletes are mostly volunteers.

Tonight, the teenage instructors are very patient as they practice a routine on the uneven parallel bars. "Okay, Greg. Go ahead," yells John, a 17-year-old high school junior who volunteers every Saturday night with his Special Olympian gymnasts. "Remember to first pull over and then do your back hip circle. Good! Now carefully go up to the high bar, do a forward roll, and then let go. All right! That looked great. Okay, Sharon. Let's see what you can do." And one after the other, the young gymnasts respond to John's words of encouragement and expertise.

Then it's on to the side horse vault. John demonstrates a squat over and then reminds the gymnasts, "Be sure to get a good jump on the board, and then keep your knees together when you tuck. Julie, go ahead. I'll be standing right here to help you." Julie smiles at John and then runs toward the horse. With her footing just a bit off, Julie slides on the launch board and runs into the horse with her chest. "You don't have to run that hard," says John. "Are you okay? Did you get hurt?" John knows that his job as a spotter is very important with these kids. You never know when they'll lose their balance or forget what they're supposed to do. Once he's sure that Julie's fine, John encourages her to try again.

Like a growing number of people his age, John is volunteering his time to a cause that he feels is important. As a handful of parents watch from the balcony overlooking the practice area, it's obvious that John is not only instructing, but having a great time, too.

"Bye John, see you next week," yells a gymnast after the session is over.

"Bye, see you next week," yells John to the group as they leave for the evening. As a huge grin spreads over his face, John admits, "I do it because I love it to death. I love it more than anything; it's what I live for. On Saturday afternoon, I'm sitting at work saying, 'I can't wait for the Special Olympics practice.' "

As someone who has been involved in gymnastics, this type of volunteering came easy to John. After three years of helping at the gym and working at a summer camp for the handicapped, John seems as motivated as ever to continue teaching others what he knows.

"We have this every Saturday night from 6:00 to 8:00 p.m.," he says as he pulls his hair away from his eyes. "We have two classes; the first class is the younger kids ages 7 to 14, and also we have different levels within the age groups."

The group John just finished with is the older group. "They're more advanced than the others," he explains. "Those were some pretty impressive routines on the uneven parallel bars."

John began working with the Special Olympians by chance. "In eighth grade my social studies teacher was pulling names from a jar to decide who would help teach the Special Olympic athletes at the high school. My name got picked," says John with a laugh. The combination of his gymnastics background with his willingness to volunteer were a perfect match!

Although John became involved in helping Special Olympians by chance, the truth is, he experienced several events in his life that made him realize volunteering was for him.

"I've always wanted to work with people. I remember I wanted to do sign language when I was younger," says John. "Then I got a chance to baby-sit for a boy who had multiple handicaps and severe mental retardation."

John baby-sat for Mark for a year until his family moved away. At that point, John was convinced he wanted to continue helping others like Mark. That was three years ago, and since then John has found many ways to help. Each summer, John spends seven weeks volunteering at a camp for mentally handicapped young adults. Like any counselor, John teaches arts and crafts, swimming, basketball and daily exercise routines. But his greatest accomplishment is the friendships he makes with young people who love his genuine concern and easygoing manner.

Where does a 17-year-old, with a part-time job and aspirations of becoming a special education teacher, find time to volunteer? "Well," says John, "it's easy if you enjoy what you're doing."

John yells "hello" to a group of friends who are waiting patiently for him at the doors of the gym. They pick him up almost every Saturday night. Apparently volunteering doesn't interfere with John's social life. "My friends like to stop by and watch what's going on," he says. "They talk with the gymnasts and have some fun."

A number of John's friends joined him earlier in the week in an experience that combined his two favorite volunteer activities: helping the handicapped and participating in his church youth group. "My youth group organized a mass for the handicapped," he explains. "One of my friends sang the song 'Wind Beneath My Wings' in sign language. She had everyone crying, including our handicapped guests. I didn't know there were so many people with disabilities in my parish, but I met a lot of them that night, and we all had a lot of fun. It was so great to have two of my favorite things right there in one place."

When asked to give a little advice to teens who are considering volunteering, John thinks for a moment and then says, "Contact a volunteer organization that interests you and see what they're doing. Just try it and give it a shot."

As John leaves the gymnasium, now dark and quiet, his friends remind him that it's time for some fun.

"Hey, John. Come on!"

After all, Saturday night is still Saturday night, even for a teen who volunteers.

Chapter Six

Protecting the Environment

Environmental problems have become perhaps the most publicized topics of this decade. Ecological dilemmas are discussed in classrooms and households, on television and radio, in newspapers and magazines and within local, state, federal and global legislative bodies. The protection of our streams, oceans, forests, wildlife, air and water has become a national project with thousands of citizens of all ages getting involved. The range of volunteer opportunities available to you is so large that if you have an interest in joining this nationwide movement, your only difficulty will be choosing which part of the environment you'd like to protect first.

Why get involved?

The reasons teens volunteer to protect the environment are as varied as the environmental groups they can work with. Some teens have said:

- *"I love nature and wildlife."*
- *"The protection of the environment is a very worthy cause that affects not only my generation, but my kids and their kids."*
- *"Recently, someone proposed putting a landfill in my town. This made me realize that environmental concerns are not somebody else's problems; they affect everyone. I volunteer because if a problem affects me, I want to do something about it."*
- *"Some of the things I enjoy, like camping, canoeing and hiking, are part of my volunteer job. So not only am I doing things I like, but I'm working to save the environment."*
- *"My older sister is in college, and she always talks about how important it is for everyone to participate to help keep our earth clean."*
- *"My family doesn't go to the shore anymore because my parents say the water is too polluted. This makes me angry. So I thought maybe there was something I could do about it."*
- *"I love nature, and I'm pretty sure that I would like to have a career that somehow protects the environment. But I have no idea exactly what I'd like to do. I thought volunteering could help me make up my mind. I'll be attending college soon, and I'd like to study something that will prepare me for the field I want to enter."*

In the future

If you think you might like a career that involves environmental protection—you'll have many professions to choose from. The need for people trained in environmental issues is widespread, and the number of fields that can prepare you for a career focused on the environment are vast. While the list is massive, here is a sample of some environment-related fields and the issues they will address in the future:

- **Biology (zoology, botany, entomology).** Biologists will study the changes in the water, air, land and animals. They'll keep us informed about the improvements and problems the earth experiences through the years.
- **Chemistry.** Chemists will invent new nontoxic materials to combat the hazardous waste problem.
- **Engineering.** Engineers will discover ways to mine, produce and use natural fuels without waste and without atmospheric damage.
- **Law.** Lawyers will fight for our right to clean water, air and land.
- **Politics.** Our elected leaders will enact the laws that protect the earth and its wildlife.
- **Education.** Educators will teach the next generation to care for our planet.

If any of these fields are of interest to you, try to focus your volunteer efforts in that particular area. Here's how:

A diverse field

The field of environmental protection certainly is diverse. That's why, before you start volunteering your time, it's important to first decide which area best matches your abilities and interests.

First, pick an aspect of the environment that's of special concern to you. Here is a list that might help you make your decision:

- **Rivers, streams, oceans.** It's estimated that 14 billion pounds of trash are dumped into the sea every year. On one occasion, volunteer cleanup crews around America picked up two million pounds of shoreline debris in just three hours!

- **Wildlife.** Extinctions are accelerating worldwide. Our planet is now losing up to three species every day.
- **Forests, tree preservation.** According to the Save A Tree organization, it takes an entire forest (more than 500,000 trees) to supply Americans with their Sunday newspapers each week. The average American uses the equivalent of seven trees a year—that's more than 1.5 billion trees used annually in the U.S.
- **Air pollution.** Almost 20 years after the Clean Air Act, tens of millions of Americans still breathe dirty air. According to the Environmental Protection Agency, more than 76 million people live in areas where the clean air standard is violated.
- **Drinking water pollution.** Nearly 117 million citizens rely on ground water for their drinking water. It's no wonder that the discovery of ground water contamination in every single state has generated much concern.
- **Preservation of natural resources.** The U.S. uses 450 billion gallons of water every day. The average U.S. home uses the energy equivalent of 1,253 gallons of oil each year. The amount of heat lost through American windows each winter is the energy equivalent of all the oil flowing through the Alaskan pipeline in a year.
- **Global problems such as ozone depletion, greenhouse effect and tropical rain forest destruction.** For the first time in history, human activities are altering the climate of our entire planet. In less than two centuries, humans have increased the total amount of carbon dioxide in the atmosphere by 25 percent.

You can see that there are many aspects of the environment that need to be protected. After you're sure that one of these is an issue you'd like to learn more about, you can decide exactly what you'd like to do to help the cause. Most volunteers who work to protect the environment do one of three kinds of jobs: clerical office work, education or hands-on projects. Take a look at what each of these jobs involves.

Staying in the office

While the purpose of all environmental groups is to protect and/or preserve our environment, this task involves a lot more than planting trees or cleaning local streams. As in any business, a lot of the necessary work takes places in offices.

Should you want to do office work, here are some of the things you might do.

- Answer phones.
- Do public contact work like verifying appointments, asking for donations and recruiting more volunteers.
- Organize or participate in fund raising.
- Assist with research.
- Give administrative support like writing press releases or running errands for others in the office.
- Participate in letter writing campaigns to the president, senators and other elected officials.

Letter writing is a small part of what is known as lobbying. Lobbying is an attempt to influence lawmakers to vote on certain issues the way your group would like. The importance of lobbying for environmental protection cannot be underestimated. It is the vital and often time-consuming job of thousands of volunteers who influence lawmakers through their letters and phone calls, as well as at rallies, demonstrations and marches.

If you like the idea of protecting the environment by working in an office or by lobbying, there are many organizations listed in the Directory that need your help. But before you call, you should take a good look at yourself to see if you have what it takes to be happy and effective in this area of work. You should be able to:

- Work well with people.
- Speak clearly and succinctly.
- Write well.
- Deal with people in a courteous, patient, appreciative and realistic manner while keeping a politely persistent attitude.
- Enjoy working behind a desk.

Justin Anderson, a 17-year-old who volunteers for Defenders of Wildlife, has participated in telephone fund raisers for his organization. He agrees that it's important to know how to deal with people. "Sometimes it's so frustrating. Most people on the telephone assume we're some radical group trying to take their money. Patience is key in dealing with them. The worst thing I could do would be to act impolite—even if it was what I really wanted to do."

Fifteen-year-old Samantha Polinski agrees. She volunteers for Greenpeace USA and is involved in letter-writing campaigns. She remembers her first frustrating experience: "The first letter I wrote was to my senator, and it was about water pollution. I received a photocopied reply about drugs. I was so mad. The only thing I could do was just keep trying."

Teaching others

Environmentalists know that to be successful, they must educate the general population. Volunteers can protect and preserve the earth by teaching others how ecological problems are caused and showing them how to become part of the solution.

Seventeen-year-old Kristy Long volunteers for a project called Kids to Kids through her high school ecology club. This program lets teens go into third-grade classrooms four times during the school year to present a 45-minute lesson. Topics for these lessons include recycling, waste reduction and energy conservation. Sometimes the student teachers hand out worksheets and coloring projects; other times they just talk. But the goal is always the same: Make young kids aware that they can have a direct effect on the planet.

"These kids seem to look up to us," says Kristy. "And very often they'll do whatever we tell them to do—maybe they'll talk their parents into recycling, or they'll run the tap water a little less." Every little bit helps, and if you teach younger children to respect this planet—who knows? The lessons you teach today may be passed on from family to family, year after year. And in the end, you will have made a big difference in the quality of life we enjoy on earth."

If you think you're interested in teaching, you may want to volunteer in several areas:

- You might train with professionals and then go into elementary school classrooms as a part of a team, teaching the importance of an environmental issue such as energy conservation. You'll teach children what they and their families can do to help.
- You can assist in the publication of environmental awareness literature.
- You might like being a tour guide for a preserved park in your area.
- It's fun to organize awareness or action projects in your school or community through an environmental agency such as those listed in the Directory. Local organizations like chambers of commerce, the Rotary and the Lions Club can often give you support to do this.
- You might create a local chapter of a national group such as Kids Against Pollution (KAP). This organization helps teens fight pollution in their home towns and gives instructions and materials to teach others how to help. This growing group of young adults was among those responsible for pressuring McDonalds into banning its non-biodegradable foam containers.

In whatever way you find yourself teaching about environmental protection, you'll find that those who do this type of volunteer work tend to share certain characteristics. Among them are:

- The ability to deal with people
- The patience and temperament to work with children
- Persistence and independence
- The ability to lead by example

Eileen O'Grady, a 15-year-old who is active in Kids Against Pollution, recalls an embarrassing moment that stresses the importance of leading by example. "My group had given third-graders a lesson in the importance of recycling. About a week later I was at the town fair, and I guess I wasn't really thinking, because I threw my soda can into the garbage. Then this little girl comes up to me and says, 'I thought you told us we should recycle soda cans.' I was so embarrassed, but I really learned a lesson."

Hands-on involvement

The third way you can volunteer to help protect the environment is to participate in the cleaning, protecting and restoration of our natural resources. This type of work is probably the most diverse and necessary. Environmentalists can write letters to congressional leaders, educate their peers and contribute to countless other efforts, but the environment, after all, is outside. Without able bodies to perform the necessary outdoor tasks, the other efforts would fall short of their goal.

If you want to do some hands-on volunteering, you'll find there are plenty of things you can do. To name just a few of the most popular teen projects, you might become involved in:

- **Recycling projects**. These projects often include placing and monitoring recycling bins in the schools, staffing the town recycling center on Saturday mornings and picking up recyclables from shut-ins.
- **Tree planting**. You might distribute seedlings to Scout troops or plant trees around your school.
- **Preservation of nature preserves**. Volunteers are often needed to clear away leaves or debris from trails, maintain bridge structures and trim forest growth.
- **Litter control/cleanup**. You might identify an area in need and organize a cleanup team, or volunteer for beach and river cleanup campaigns.
- **Energy conservation projects**. Such projects often include making and distributing signs that remind others to turn off lights and running water, organizing drives to encourage mass transportation, walking and bike riding instead of using cars and arranging student car pools to school.

- **Pollution site identification**. Volunteer groups test and record water and air samples.
- **Storm drain stenciling**. This includes painting pictures of fish on roadside storm drains, reminding others that everything that goes down a drain eventually runs into waterways and oceans.
- **Waterway protection**. Volunteers might organize a stream cleanup to remove debris that pollutes water and prohibits fish from going upstream to spawn, get involved in stream monitoring programs or stabilize stream banks by planting willows and other woody plants

Just as there are many kinds of environmental projects, there are many kinds of people well-suited to this work. However, hands-on volunteer work is most rewarding for certain kinds of people:

- **People who love to be outside**. The job of protecting the environment happens in all kinds of weather—sun, rain, snow and wind. In some cases you can pick the region of the country and the season in which you will be working, but Mother Nature is unpredictable.

  Cindy Lee, a 17-year-old who volunteers for the Touch America Project through the U.S. Department of Agriculture Forest Service, spends her volunteering hours maintaining trails in a national park. She says, "I love being outside whatever the weather is like. Even though the weather is nice most of the time, I wouldn't advise this type of work to someone who doesn't love being outdoors."
- **People who don't mind getting dirty**. Hands-on volunteering can send you home looking like you've been mud wrestling. This might be a bit of an exaggeration, but the point is: you need to be willing to put on a pair of old jeans and get your hands dirty. Maintaining wildlife sanctuaries for the National Audubon Society, for example, may involve general cleanup of an outdoor trail or cleaning, feeding and caring for animals. Both tasks will certainly leave you dirtier than writing letters of petition.

- **People who have an aptitude or interest in manual labor**. This quality is necessary if your job is going to involve restoration or maintenance work. For instance, if you find yourself volunteering for the Student Conservation Association, Inc., you will be responsible for trail maintenance, bridge building and/or general restoration of protected wilderness areas.
- **People who appreciate immediate results**. Hands-on work can be difficult and challenging, but the rewards are immediate and positive. Hands-on volunteers are concerned with a specific project that needs to be done now. The only factor that determines success is their own personal effort. This gives the volunteer a real sense of self-worth and satisfaction.

  Steve Pritchett, a 16-year-old volunteer who spends his time involved in coastal cleanups through the Natural Guard, shares this feeling. "When I finish a day of volunteering," he says, "I feel good because I know I made a difference. It's a difference that I can look at and say that I'm doing my share to help out. And the difference is visible."

Think you have what it takes to do hands-on volunteering? Well, if you're not sure, you might want to give it a try anyway. Sometimes you can't be sure about the fulfillment of physical work until you do it. Gigna Patel, a 15-year-old who also volunteers at coastal cleanups with the Natural Guard, is a perfect example. "I went to my first coastal cleanup," Gigna remembers, "because my friends were going. When I found out what I had to do, I thought I wasn't going to like it at all. But by the end of the day, I was actually happy I had gone, and now I volunteer all the time."

How much time do you have?

The opportunities for volunteering in this field are so plentiful that you should be able to find a project suited to your schedule. Some organizations have programs that need volunteer help only a few times a year. These include seasonal educational programs, cleanup task forces and letter-writing campaigns to influence votes on particular environmental legislation. Other programs run for a few consecutive months each year—usually during the summer. These programs include those offered by the Student Conservation Association, Inc. Volunteers live and work for four weeks in wilderness areas, maintaining trails and restoring wildlife preserves.

As you're deciding where to volunteer, remember to consider how much time you have to offer. Some organizations need a firm commitment while others appreciate any amount of time and may arrange a schedule to fit your needs. Be sure to ask.

Starting your own group

Many teens across the country have started environmental programs in their communities. They've established recycling programs, cleaned parks and waterways, organized letter-writing campaigns, developed energy conservation plans, created puppet shows and plays to teach young kids about environmental protection and written and taught classroom lessons. While the process involves more of a commitment on your part, the rewards can be equally great.

Established organizations can give your grassroots project a boost. Some may even help you start a local chapter. Read over the list of organizations in the Directory and see if there's one that might be able to help you get started. Then give them a call and find out. Also, don't forget to read Chapter Eight to find out exactly how to get your project off the ground.

To get an idea of the kind of work you might expect to do, read the following story of a typical day for one volunteer, Tracy Van Hise.

Working to protect and preserve nature: Tracy Van Hise

The blaring alarm clock and insistent phone force Tracy Van Hise towards another Saturday at the nature center. Shutting the alarm clock, which now reads 7:31 a.m., Tracy fumbles for the telephone.

"Hello," she answers wearily.

"Good morning, Tracy. This is Steve from the center. Sorry to wake you, sleepyhead, but I need to know if you'll have your car here today."

"Umm, I think so. Well, I don't know. I mean, I will unless my mother needs the car today. Why?"

"I don't know how long I'll be here today, and in case there are any pickups, I wanted to make sure someone would have a car."

"Okay. I'll see what I can do."

"Great. I'll see you in a bit. Oh, Tracy, one more thing. Put on your old clothes because it looks like it's going to be a dirty day."

"You got it. I'll see you later."

Steve runs the county nature center where Tracy volunteers every Saturday. He's also responsible for two other centers in the area. Since Tracy, at the age of 17, is the oldest volunteer, she has become second-in-charge. Tracy likes the responsibility. After three years of being at the center, she takes pride in being a veteran.

After washing up and changing into her "work" clothes, Tracy heads downstairs. Her mother has a bowl of cereal and a glass of orange juice waiting for her.

"Do you need the car today, Mom?" Tracy asks.

"Why? Is this another one-car day for the nature center?"

"Steve called to say that he may not be there all day and asked me if I could bring the car in case of a pickup call."

"Okay. You can take the car. Remember to pick up Mark, and make sure you both wear your seat belts."

"Sure, Mom. Thanks. I'll see you later."

Tracy goes out the back door into the nippy air of a September morning. It rained last night, and the sound of her boots squishing in the mud makes her glad she wore her old clothes. She opens the back of her mother's station wagon and lays out the beat-up blankets to prepare for any pickups. With a quick glance at her watch which reads 8:03 a.m., she jumps into the car and backs out of the driveway.

The nature center is a natural preserve located on about five acres of land. It's filled with paths and benches and is often visited by locals who enjoy spending the day outside. In the last two years, Tracy and the other volunteers have started working on an exciting project. They're making wooden information stands to place along the trail. These stands hold a written description of the different kinds of trees, plants and wildlife visitors can see. The volunteers are hoping that these stands will enable visitors to leave the center with more knowledge about the environment. Also, since this project began, the center has become a popular spot for elementary school children on field trips. Tracy is glad to see this because she believes that teaching younger kids about the environment is a very important part of her job.

The center also houses an injured bird shelter. This is where Tracy spends most of her time. The volunteers are taught how to care for and treat injured birds. Sometimes concerned citizens bring these birds to the center; other times they're pickups. "Pickup" is the term center volunteers use for a phone call regarding an injured bird. A volunteer drives to the location and brings the bird back to the shelter.

Tracy pulls up in front of Mark's house and beeps the horn. It's 8:25 a.m.; she's five minutes early. Tracy waits in the car and a few minutes later, Mark bounds through his front door. Mark is an energetic 14-year-old who just started volunteering at the nature center about two months ago. Tracy likes working with Mark. He's full of energy, and he looks up to Tracy. He is also full of questions.

Marks jumps into the passenger seat. "Hey, Tracy. What's up? What are we going to do today? Any pickups? Is Steve going to be there? Do you think we'll get..."

"Whoa. Hold on Mark. It's too early for me to play 20 questions. Let's get to the center and take it from there, okay?"

"Okay, Tracy. But hey, I was just wondering...can I feed the sparrow today?"

Tracy and Mark pull up to the center right at 9:00 a.m. Just as they're getting out of the car, Steve comes out of the bird shelter.

"Good morning, Tracy. Hey, Mark. Ready to work today, big guy?"

"Yes sir! Are there any pickups today? Did you feed the sparrow yet? Can I..."

"Can you clean out the cages? Good idea, kiddo. Why don't you get on that now. Those poor birds are living in some pretty smelly stuff."

"Okay. Then can I feed the sparrow?"

"Sure. Clean first, okay? I have to talk to Tracy for a minute."

"What's up, Steve? Anything wrong?" asks Tracy.

"No. It's just that I really can't hang around today. There is a lot of work to be done, and Peresh and Marcie aren't coming in today. So you're going to be a little understaffed. Just do your best, and I'll see you next Saturday."

"Okay. See ya," Tracy says as Steve pulls away in his car.

Tracy goes into the shelter to check on Mark. Cleaning the cages is the chore usually given to the "rookie." As Tracy walks into the room, she vividly remembers why this is a rookie chore. The room smells awful. But it doesn't seem to bother Mark at all.

"How does that cage look, Tracy? I already cleaned his cage. Is he named already? Because if he's not, I want to name him Oscar."

"Oscar it is, Mark. Yes, you're doing a very good job. But why don't you put on the rubber gloves?"

"Oh yeah. I forgot. Which cage should I clean next?"

"Mark, you can do them in any order you want. They all have to be cleaned."

"All of them?" asks Mark, his enthusiasm dwindling.

"Yes, Mark. But Susan and Gary should be here soon. They..."

"You called?" Susan asks, as she and Gary enter and start putting on their rubber gloves.

"Hi, guys," answers Tracy. "I'm going to go outside and finish up the stand we were working on last week. Can you help Mark clean the cages and then feed the birds?" she asks as she grabs a hammer and heads outside.

"Uh...the sparrow?" Mark yells after Tracy to remind her of her promise.

Tracy laughs. "Oh, yeah. Let Mark feed the sparrow."

Tracy makes her rounds and then spends an hour finishing the new stand. As she stands and looks around, she's surprised to see a family walking along the trails already. Tracy watches from a distance as the father reads aloud from one of the stands while his wife and their two kids listen closely. Tracy breathes in the fresh air, feeling very satisfied, and then heads off to finish another stand.

After she completes the second stand, Tracy looks at her watch—12:14 p.m. She laughs to herself as she thinks how long it would have taken her to put up the stands a few years ago. Her first experience with a hammer was certainly a challenging one. As a rookie, she helped with a bridge restoration project, and she remembers that it took her more than an hour to hammer one board on correctly. Tracy then realizes that she should be getting back to the shelter to see how the other volunteers are doing.

She quickens her pace as she hears loud noises and laughter coming from the house. She begins to laugh, too, when she sees Mark, Gary and Susan having a water fight with the hoses behind the bird shelter.

"Get her!" yells Gary as he spots Tracy.

It's too late for Tracy to escape. Before she knows it, she's in the middle of a water fight, soaking wet and laughing hysterically. But she stops suddenly when she hears the phone ringing. Tracy bolts inside to answer it.

"Hello...Okay. Where are you located? All right, we'll be there soon. Thank you for calling."

"Is it a pickup? Can I go with you?" Mark pleads.

"Hold your horses. I hope you guys finished the cages and the feeding before you decided to soak yourselves...and me." Tracy laughs as she looks at herself and her friends. She can't believe this place sometimes. She remembers the time when she and the volunteers were playing hide-and-go-seek after work, and Steve started a mud fight down near the stream. What a place! Mark's rambling soon brings her back to the present.

"...that one. And I cleaned that one. And I even mopped the floor. The sparrow is all fed, but its wing doesn't look like it's healing. Is he going to be okay?"

"It takes a while for wings to heal," Tracy assures him. "We can just do our best and hope it works. Well, good job. Our feathered friends look much happier now. You know, sometimes I hate to see them go when they heal."

"Oh, I almost forgot," interrupts Gary. "Steve called. He said he forgot to tell you that you can let the cardinal go today. The vet was here yesterday and said he's fine."

"Another bon voyage," Tracy says as she slips on a pair of rubber gloves.

Mark opens the cage, and Tracy gently grabs the cardinal, smoothing his wings closed. Susan opens the door, and Tracy slowly walks outside with the bird. The instant they get outside, Tracy releases her grasp, and the bird flies off into the woods. Tracy feels good. Three weeks ago that bird looked like it wasn't going to make it. There's another healthy bird flying around because of the nature center—and her.

"Gary, I need you to clean a cage for this pickup. And Susan, can you go on a cleanup hike? There were a lot of people here this week, and I'm sure they left behind some garbage."

"What about me?" asks Mark as he walks with Tracy toward the car. "Can I go with you? What kind of bird do you think it is? Can I name it? Do you think the cardinal will be okay?"

Tracy doesn't answer Mark's questions because her thoughts are on the cycle of her volunteer work. In one day, she's let a healthy bird return to nature, and she's bringing in an injured one needing loving care. It feels good to be a part of this circle of life.

Chapter Seven

Politics

If you have decided to volunteer because you want to make a difference—volunteering in politics may be just the thing for you. You can influence more aspects of American life by volunteering in the political process than in any other type of volunteering. Teen political volunteers indirectly contribute to all the fields of service mentioned in this book. The elected officials in our cities, states and nation certainly are involved in the issues affecting environmental protection, substance abuse prevention, health care, education and the needy.

As you can see, volunteering time to the political process is certainly a positive way to influence the world around you. Our country was founded on the idea that every citizen has a right to participate in the government. This right extends not only to those of legal voting age, but also to the teens of America. As voter apathy increases among the elders of our country, it is teens who, in increasing numbers, are jumping into the arena of politics and making a difference.

Why do teens choose politics?

In addition to allowing them to contribute to our community and nation, teens have mentioned other motives for volunteering. Among them are:

- *"I love politics. This is fun for me."*
- *"Volunteering helps me meet other people with similar political interests."*
- *"I would like to be a politician some day. I'm hoping that the connections I make now will help me in the future."*
- *"I'm hoping that by volunteering time to help a local political candidate, my college application will show my sense of civic duty and political awareness."*
- *"I enjoy being a leader. When I volunteer with the Young Democrats, I am constantly influencing and guiding others to register to vote and to vote for a particular candidate."*
- *"Working on a campaign for a candidate I admire lets me be part of a team. I've learned that teamwork is not only important but necessary for a successful campaign."*
- *"By volunteering I keep myself informed on important current issues."*
- *"To be honest, I'm volunteering because I'd really like to attend West Point. I'm hoping my local representative will write me a good letter of recommendation, which is a required part of the application."*

Who can volunteer in politics?

Political groups and candidates will certainly accept any help they can get during a campaign. Any volunteer between the ages of 13 and 19 is welcome. Whatever your age or talent, there's surely something you can do to help.

There are, however, certain personal characteristics that make the experience a more successful one. Among these are:

- **A sincere desire to benefit the political process**. David Tiomkin, co-chairman of his local Teenage Republican organization, knows this is important. He says, "I think political ideas form before you actually vote, so I don't think politicians should wait until kids are 18 to invite them into the party. There's a lot we can do before then."
- **A friendly and open disposition**. Campaign workers must present themselves to strangers in a way that reflects positively on the candidate. While it's not necessary for you to be a "politician" yourself, if you want to campaign you need to be able to interact with the voting public in a positive way.
- **The ability to effectively communicate**. This becomes important when making phone calls and canvassing neighborhoods. If you mumble incoherently, you will not positively influence your target audience.
- **The ability to work as a team**. A successful volunteer has a clear sense of what obligation and commitment mean. Volunteers must form an interdependent net woven from the efforts of an entire team. This team approach to politicking illustrates the old saying: "A chain is only as strong as its weakest link." In politics, a poor sense of obligation and commitment create a weak link in the candidate's chain.
- **A sincere belief in the candidate or party**. We all work best for causes we believe in. If your feelings are neutral, you may be able to do the required work, but certainly nothing more, and you won't work with vigor or excitement. Sluggish or unenthusiastic volunteering is not helpful to the candidate, the party, other volunteers or you.
- **Being informed about political candidates and issues**. There are many ways you can do this. You can read about candidates and issues in newspapers, magazines

and books. And you can listen to those who are knowledgeable about the issues. With this basic information, you can ask intelligent questions. Talk to your parents, relatives, teachers, elders in the community and citizens who are directly involved in the political process, like city officials, candidates and other volunteers.

You can also learn about candidates and legislative issues by collecting political literature. Every candidate and party has free handouts intended to positively influence your opinion. But be careful! This literature is propaganda at its best. The material is written to sway your opinions. One way to avoid being manipulated by political literature is to gather pamphlets and other papers from many sources. After you have collected material representing several different viewpoints, you can read, compare and contrast the information. You may be surprised or confused by the amount of conflicting information you're sure to find. But this is simply part of politics. If you want to be informed, it's your job to weed out misleading information and absorb what's useful and seemingly true.

- **Energy and enthusiasm**. The attitude you need to successfully volunteer in politics is very similar to the one found on the sidelines during the Super Bowl. There is a lot of cheering, supporting and behind-the-scenes work that's necessary to ensure a victory. If you give a candidate this same energy and enthusiasm, you'll be a valued member of the team.
- **An optimistic belief that the efforts of one teen volunteer can really make a difference**. As you know, the political world is enormous and complicated. Others may tell you that this "monster" will not be affected by your efforts. But what's important is what *you* think. Do you think you can make a difference by chipping in and doing your share to help a cause that you believe in? Many teens do. Seventeen-year-old Khara Bozler knows she makes a difference. She says, "Teens say we don't count, but it's not true. We can get involved and make our

contributions count. Campaigning lets me influence the outcome of elections even though I can't vote yet."

- **A desire for a political career**. If you want to be a politician someday, volunteering for a political party is a good way to start. Imagine how different American history would be if Abraham Lincoln or Franklin Delano Roosevelt never entered politics because the whole system seemed too large and intimidating. Eighteen-year-old Douglas Kammerer has already made the plunge. "I might want to run for office someday," he says. "So I want to get involved in the party at an early age. Volunteering is a way to let influential people know about my abilities."

An old adage says: "The journey of a thousand miles begins with the first step." You need to believe this to successfully volunteer in politics.

On the campaign trail

The world of politics is buzzing with action year round. But volunteers are most desperately needed in the few months before an election. Many activities begin around Labor Day and continue through to Election Day, held the first Tuesday in November.

If you volunteer during an election campaign, here are some of the things you may find yourself doing:

Working the phone bank. A phone bank is a place where there are lots of telephones. People gather to make calls promoting their candidate and political issues. The bank can be in the group's headquarters, in a local store after hours or maybe in someone's home. But wherever it is during election season, you can be sure it will be filled with volunteers.

Phone workers call people for several reasons. When election day is still a month or two away, volunteers call unregistered voters or people who will soon be eligible to vote. They call to encourage these people to register. They may also suggest that the potential voter declare a party affiliation. But the goal is simply to involve as many people as possible in the election process. With voter registration numbers so low in our country, getting even a few more voters on the books could make a notable difference.

As election day draws near, volunteers phone registered voters. They will call people registered with their own party to remind them to vote. And they'll call voters who are registered as Independents and encourage them to vote for a particular candidate or issue. Sometimes volunteers may also make phone calls to survey general public opinion.

Fund raising. A great deal of money is needed to run even a modest political campaign. Literature, posters, radio, TV and newspaper ads, transportation, food and housing cost money. Candidates often get financial support from the national political party, from local donations and from their own pockets. But they can always use more.

The more money candidates have, the more people will know about them. That's why you may find yourself washing cars or baking cakes to raise more money. This may not be what you had in mind when you offered to help a political cause, but remember: when you volunteer in politics, you join a team where everyone must be willing to help out in any way necessary. Raising money is quite often on the top of a volunteer's list.

Canvassing. Canvassing involves distributing literature door-to-door. In most cases, volunteers not only hand out pamphlets, but they also talk to residents. They give them reasons to consider voting for a particular candidate or issue. This door-to-door soliciting is usually done every Saturday beginning two months before Election Day.

This is a very important job because you come face-to-face with the voting public and you represent your candidate and his or her stance on the issues. Listen to what one volunteer had to say about her canvassing experience: "The first couple of times, a bunch of us went together because it's a little daunting to go to someone's door and talk about politics. But after the first few houses, I started feeling more relaxed, and I could talk about the candidate without feeling worried. It gets easier. But if you don't feel comfortable doing that, there's lots of other stuff you could do like mailings or phone calls or making signs."

Clerical work. Clerical work includes filing, typing, answering phones, running errands, writing, addressing, folding and mailing letters. Volunteers spend lots of time on these tasks. Although desk work can be boring in some instances, that's never the case at political headquarters. As election day draws near, the pace is fast and exhilarating.

Other volunteer activities

During campaigns, there are thousands of things that teen volunteers can do to help put their federal, state and/or local candidates over the top. In addition to the most common tasks explained above, a list of more specific activities is offered in a flier called "Working Partners" published for Teenage Republicans. Many of these are activities you can expect to find when volunteering for any political organization. They include:

- Making signs and recruiting teenagers to participate at rallies
- Distributing information on voting requirements and informing people when and where to register to vote
- Providing a baby-sitting service on Election Day
- Providing a driving service to the polls
- Conducting mock elections at school
- Setting up coffee booths at shopping centers, train stations, factories and sports events for the purpose of distributing candidate literature
- Setting up booths at local, county and state fairs to promote candidates
- Decorating campaign headquarters
- Clipping newspaper articles for candidates
- Providing transportation for visiting candidates and their families
- Working as runners and poll watchers on Election Day
- Sending postcards to voting age friends and relatives urging them to vote
- Making and distributing yard signs for candidates

- Decorating cars and floats for parades
- Copying lists of new residents in the community
- Copying lists of registered voters
- Serving as ushers and greeters at campaign events

There's no question about it. Teens are needed and welcome in any political race.

All year long

Teens who volunteer for political organizations do not necessarily work only for election campaigns. Some activities are more general and are performed all year long.

In this country we have a majority two-party system—the Republican Party and the Democratic Party. Each of these has an organized youth membership group. These teens usually meet monthly to address a variety of topics. In addition to preparing for specific activities such as voter registration drives and fund-raising activities, these teens focus on:

- **Developing ideas for recruiting new members**. The more able bodies in your group, the better. So volunteers have to find ways to spread the word about the party's philosophy and goals. Then they try to find other teens who can help them meet these goals.
- **Establishing committees and electing officers**. Political party organizations run their meetings by formal rules. While all members are young, hard-working volunteers, order and structure promote efficiency in any organization.
- **Publishing a newsletter**. Newsletters can help to motivate and reward members by publicizing their accomplishments. They may also influence the political views of others by highlighting the good work of the national party. The newsletter might be sent to members, parents and the community or to other chapters of the organization in different parts of the country.
- **Learning more about the political party**. Teen organizations offer many opportunities for learning about politics.

They arrange for guest speakers. They take trips to meet with other teen chapter members. And some visit Washington, D.C. to get a closer look at the political system at work. The more information a group has, the better prepared the members are for their work on the campaign trail. This learning process can be very enjoyable and often leads to opportunities for having fun and meeting other people with similar interests.

Most groups also participate in a variety of activities that benefit the community without any direct political goal. Teenage Republicans and Young Democrats groups across the country have volunteered in activities such as these:

- Sponsoring food and clothing drives for underprivileged families
- Providing tutoring services for younger children
- Sending Christmas cards to servicemen stationed in other countries
- Working with local student groups such as Students Against Driving Drunk (SADD)
- Assisting with protection programs such as Crime Watch or Neighborhood Watch
- Participating in programs such as Meals on Wheels and blood drives
- Sponsoring holiday events for underprivileged children
- Participating in fund raisers for nonprofit organizations
- Sponsoring local youth groups such as sports teams
- Acting as peer listeners
- Holding child fingerprinting/identification sessions at area schools
- Assisting the elderly with yard work and chores
- Collecting toys for needy children and area pediatric centers

As you can see, volunteering for a political organization is not all "political." There are many opportunities for you to get involved in your city, state and nation on both a political and social level.

Getting started

Want to volunteer in politics? Well, if it's election time, you can call your local party headquarters. To find it, ask an information operator or call the national headquarters listed in the Directory.

While the offices will be in dire need of your services between Labor Day and Election Day, you can get involved at any time of the year. Just call or write the headquarters listed in the Directory and ask for information on the youth group in your area. If there isn't one nearby, a representative from the national office will be glad to help you start one.

When you volunteer in politics, every day brings new challenges and surprises. But some days can be quite exceptional in this high profile field. Take a look at how Ron Poliquin spent one of his days as a volunteer with the Teenage Republicans.

A profile of a teen political volunteer: Ron Poliquin

Rrrrring... Rrrrring...

"Hello," mumbles Ron sleepily into the phone.

"Ron, sorry to call so early, but I just wanted to let you know that 10 kids have signed up to hang campaign signs tomorrow for the Congressman. Can you come?"

"Yeah, Mike. I'll be there," says Ron as he hangs up and rolls over in bed to peek at the clock.

It's 8 o'clock on Saturday morning. For most of his life, Ron Poliquin slept late on Saturdays. But for the last two years, his position as chairman of the local Teenage Republicans chapter has nudged him out of bed at this early hour. There's always so much to do.

Swinging his legs to the floor, Ron reaches again for the phone. He'll make two calls before he's even washed his face this morning. First Ron calls the secretary at his congressman's office.

"Hello, Mr. Morris? This is Ron Poliquin," he begins. "I just wanted to let you know that we have about 10 kids who've volunteered to help hang signs tomorrow. We're meeting at noon in the parking lot behind your building."

"Great, Ron," says George Morris. "I was hoping you'd be able to help out. Do you need anything?"

"No, thanks. I have the signs in my father's car, and I've made a map that divides up the town among us, so I think I'm all set. See you tomorrow."

Ron hangs up and dials again.

"Hi, Jenn. I just wanted to remind you to send out those welcome letters to our new members. Be sure to mention that we're going to meet in front of the school to distribute campaign literature next weekend. The more people we can get, the more ground we'll cover. I've got to run now or I'm gonna be late. See ya later."

Ron is off to Republican Headquarters where he's volunteered to help prepare for a senatorial candidate's press conference. This candidate is bidding to become the state's first Republican senator in 22 years, and the party is very excited to have him meet the press in their town.

It's 9:30 a.m., and Ron is the second to arrive. The first was Judy Fow, the secretary of the county's Republican Committee. Judy is delighted to see Ron's face because there's so much to be done in this large, drab room to prepare for the party they'll throw after the press conference. Ron wastes no time. He throws his jacket in the corner, pushes up his sleeves and starts hauling folded tables across the floor. More volunteers arrive, and the work moves smoothly. They dust and vacuum, set up more tables and chairs, test the sound system and make place cards for their special guests. They blow up balloons and string up red, white and blue streamers. They hang signs, and pass out campaign buttons. Everyone keeps an eye on the courthouse across the street, where a crowd is gathering, waiting for the candidate. The excitement in the room grows with the arrival of each new prominent legislator. Assemblymen, freeholders and council members are all gathering in front of the old court house.

After a short while, this feeling of excitement begins to turn to nervousness. The candidate is a half-hour late, and the crowd is getting anxious. Before she gets on the phone to track down the problem, Judy Fow asks Ron to go across the street and tell the legislators and others not to worry because the candidate will be there soon.

Ron knows it's important that he appears calm and confident as he delivers this message (which he is not at all sure is true). With a big smile and a handshake, Ron approaches his state assemblyman and county freeholder and assures them that the press conference will begin soon. He delivers the same message to the members of the media, who are pacing and checking their watches every few seconds. Ron walks through the crowd making more assurances and growing more worried, when off in the distance Ron spots it—the candidate's campaign van! With a very audible sigh of relief, Ron runs back to headquarters to alert the other volunteers. "The press conference is ready to begin," he yells. "The next senator of this state has just arrived!" With a collective cheer, the group runs out to hear the candidate's speech.

Ron stays behind with Judy. There's still a lot to be done before the party. He goes out back to meet the caterer's truck and carries in platters of breads, cold cuts, salads and cookies. He brings out the plates, cups, forks, spoons and knives. As Judy arranges the food, Ron sets up the coffee pots, all the while keeping an eye on the action across the street. "Here they come!" he warns Judy, as the Republican delegation heads back toward headquarters.

As the crowd comes in, Ron begins the work he likes best—talking with politicians. He sees Oscar Brooks, a councilman up for reelection, by the punch bowl. After introducing himself and commenting briefly on the candidate's speech, Ron asks Mr. Brooks if the Teenage Republicans might be able to help him in his campaign. Oscar Brooks is thrilled. He knows that teens can offer to a campaign the enthusiasm and optimism he's been looking for. Ron makes a mental note to call the councilman during the week.

Judy politely interrupts their conversation to ask Ron if he'd please get more soda from the kitchen. With two arms full of soda bottles, Ron closes the refrigerator door with his foot and bumps into the senatorial candidate's wife. After giving his apologies, Ron introduces himself and offers best wishes for the candidate's election. "I'm so glad to meet you," she says with a broad smile. "My husband and I appreciate all the many things your club has done for this campaign. We really believe that the support of young people like you is crucial to our success. I encourage you to keep up the good work." With these words echoing in his ears, Ron returns to the party with the soda. Sometimes he wonders if his efforts really make any difference, then a simple comment like this lets him know his work is really important.

As the autumn sun eases down below the horizon, the Republican headquarters stands empty once again. The party's over. The streamers lie trampled on the floor. The balloons are scattered around the room. Plates of half-eaten sandwiches and cups of cold coffee sit on tables as silent reminders of what went on here today. As Ron gathers up the trash and sweeps the floor, he thinks back over the hard work he's put into the political process. He has no doubt it's all worth it, because what's happening right now will directly affect his generation. And he wants to have a say in that.

Chapter Eight

Doing It Yourself

Although the work of volunteering is not always easy to do, for many programs, joining up is as simple as saying, "I'd like to help." Well-established organizations may have headquarters phone numbers, recruiting programs or sign-up sheets in your local school or church. All you need to do is say that you're interested, and it's likely that you'll soon be an official volunteer.

But what if you have an idea that's not already being done? What if you see a project that needs exactly what you and your friends think you can provide? What if you want to start your own volunteer organization? This chapter will help get you started.

What do you want to do?

First, you'll need to ask yourself some crucial questions: What exactly do I hope to accomplish with this idea? For example, if I see garbage on the playground, do I want my group to clean it up? Do I want it kept clean? Do I want to draw public attention to the problem? Do I want public attention for the project? Do I have friends who will help? What's my deadline for doing it? Will it cost money? How will I get it? These questions could apply to almost any project you attempt.

Gather information

Once you set a specific goal for your project, start talking. Talk to your friends, your parents, your teachers, your neighbors—anyone who will listen to your ideas. Jot down their reactions and their suggestions. Keep everything in a file folder. Don't let negative responses discourage you—sometimes honest criticism can help lead to a better idea.

Has anyone done anything like this project? To find out, call an already-established organization and ask. The Directory will give you the names of groups that cover a wide range of volunteer projects. Call and ask for their local or county directors. Then call these people, explain your proposal and ask if they have any ideas that might help you get started. Are you willing to join forces with another organization? If so, this may be your opportunity to start a new branch in your area. If not, be ready to politely decline any offer or invitation to combine efforts.

With help from your friends

An important factor to keep in mind, even at this early stage, is the need for support. Even the most enthusiastic people can lose momentum if they feel they're doing everything alone. Try to find a partner or a small group to help you. This way, if one of you begins to suffer from burnout, there will be someone else around to keep the flame going.

Once you've come up with a good idea, gathered information and gained the support of some friends, what's next? It's time to prepare for your first meeting.

When can you meet?

You have to plan a date and time for your meeting. Grab a calendar and sit down with your friends. It's a good idea to find a calendar that lists holidays and school vacations, and then make a copy of the upcoming months. Pick a target week when you'd like to begin, and keep in mind activities you're already committed to. Remember to consider when that English paper is due, when SATs are scheduled, or which weekend is the big dance. Put an X through each day where a one- to two-hour chunk of time is not available. Look over what's left and decide on your first choice. (Don't worry about where you'll meet or who will supervise; you'll cross those bridges later.) Pick about three or four alternate dates and choose a time frame for each date as well. List these clearly on a memo to yourself.

Where can you meet?

You'll need a place to meet. Ask yourself: Does it have to be a homey and comfortable place? Is it available evenings and daytime? Is it easily accessible to everyone? Does it have the equipment I need (table or desk, chairs, blackboard, easel or telephone)? Can it be in someone's home?

Make sure you'll have enough space for everyone to gather and be heard. Overflowing crowds may give the appearance of enthusiastic support for an idea, but any group can become easily sidetracked if all participants are not able to hear and speak. If your home is too small, consider a church meeting room or a high school classroom.

You'll need to call the facilities director to ask about availability. Be sure to have all the information about your project ready before you dial the telephone. In fact, it may be a good idea to practice this conversation with a friend. See how something like the following script sounds:

"Hello, my name is ________, and I'm starting a volunteer program to help ________. We need a place to meet during the week of ________, and we'd like to know if you have a room where we can begin our work. We'd like to meet on __________ at ___________ o'clock."

Try to have an estimate of how many people you expect. Know if you'll have adult supervision. And estimate how long you'll need the room. Remember: Be prepared before you dial the phone.

Adult supervision

If the facility will not allow you to meet without adult supervision, consider inviting an adult to volunteer his or her time. Try the obvious choices: your mom, dad, an interested teacher or guidance counselor. But don't overlook the retired lady who sits in front of you at church, or the crossing guard whose after school and evening hours may be free. Think about neighbors who know you because you baby sit their children or cut their lawns. They already know you're reliable and may be willing to help.

Still stuck? Call a local church or two and ask them for ideas, or see if they'll print your request in their weekly bulletin. Try the senior citizens' organization. Do you know any local college kids who may be studying in the field of your service project? As long as they're over legal age and have taken a minimum number of college credits (the number is different from state to state), they qualify as coaches or substitute teachers, and that's good enough to be a group supervisor. All this searching serves more than one purpose: It gives you and your project visibility at the same time that you're solving the practical problem of finding meeting space.

Recruiting members

Well, you're on your way; you have a starting date and time, and you have a place for your first meeting. Congratulations! Now you need people. How do you want to let everyone know about your kick-off meeting? Try these ideas:

- Advertise in your school. Does your school allow posters or fliers to be hung or distributed? Does it have an electronic bulletin board?
- Don't overlook your church or synagogue. Will local religious organizations print a blurb in their bulletins or newsletters?
- Use the local newspaper. Would they print a sentence or two on their "Here's What's Going On" page?
- Look for stores that have community bulletin boards where you can hang a small poster or flier.
- Call local radio and cable TV stations. Tell them about your idea, and ask if they can help you publicize the first meeting.
- Do something wild. Do you know anyone with a private plane that can tow a sign? Skywriters? A hot air balloon? A van with a speaker on top like political candidates use?

Keep thinking and dreaming. You never know who will come out to help.

Preparing for your first meeting

Now that you have a date, time and place to meet with lots of committed volunteers, you can just sit back and wait for it to happen...right? *No!* Your first meeting is crucial. Here are some tips to make it so special everyone will want to come back, do wonderful things for your cause and bring all their friends to help. Try these:

1. Build in the fun. Nobody wants to work all the time, even if they believe strongly in the work. So build some fun into your meeting.

- **Plan snacks**. For the first meeting, provide them yourself, or get a friend or your parents to help. Have a sign-up sheet prominently placed for snack volunteers, and ask for phone numbers so that they can be reminded. Keep it simple, but make it an important part of your meetings. Some groups like to take a break and snack; others prefer to munch while they work. Do what's best for your group, and make sure you clean up.

- **Plan an icebreaker activity.** This may or may not have anything to do with your project. The main purpose is to get people talking to each other, ease the tension a bit and have fun. Here are some examples:

  Get acquainted. Make up a list of about 20 questions like these:

  Who in this group has a parent who grew up in this town?
  Who in this group has lived in another state?
  Who in this group has blue eyes?
  Who in this group likes math?
  Who in this group has a younger brother or sister?

  Give each person a paper and pencil. Why not offer a simple inexpensive prize for the first person done?

  Name game. Each person thinks of an adjective that begins with the same letter as his or her first name. Then each person introduces him or herself using the adjective with his or her name, for example, "Hi. I'm Lovable Laura," or "Hi. I'm Silly Steve."

  Shuffle your buns. To begin this activity, everyone sits in a circle. There should be enough chairs for all but one person. The extra person stands in the middle and says something like, "Everyone who's wearing red, shuffle your buns." Then all players wearing red must move to a new seat. They can't return to their original chair or to one right next to it. The person left standing chooses the next characteristic for "shuffling." When everyone seems to be comfortable and relaxed, ask them to gather so that you can begin the meeting.

2. Build in structure. Creating the structure of your organization will require some advanced planning. To develop an idea about how you might structure your project, ask yourself these questions:

- Do we need officers? How many? What will their responsibilities be?
- Do we want to have formal meetings? To get an idea of how parliamentary procedure works at formal meetings, get a copy of *Roberts' Rules of Order* from your library.
- If we want to remain informal, what are the goals and objectives we need to meet at each meeting? Should we plan an agenda?
- Will we need a constitution or bylaws? Complicated as this may sound, many schools won't allow you to meet as a school group until you file a formal statement of organization. This formal statement may also be useful when you need to raise money or open a bank account and also when you need advice.
- How are we going to involve our adult sponsor if we have one?
- Will we need committees? You can't do all the work yourself, so learn to divide up responsibilities.

Another tip: Practice using the word "we." As the originator or founder of the group, you do have a lot to say about the structure of your organization. But you probably want to avoid sounding or acting like a dictator. Use the word "we" instead of "I" when you talk to your group and make assignments.

3. Make an agenda. Plan your meeting agenda in advance. It doesn't have to be elaborate (an example follows), and it can be shared with the group in one of two ways:

1. Print the agenda and make copies. Give one to each member so they can use it for notes and reminders of future events.
2. If you can't copy your agenda, print it on large poster paper (using a marker pen) and tape it on a wall where everyone can see it. As you complete items, check them off. Write in any important decisions the group makes

right on the paper. At the end of the meeting, you or the secretary can take it home and summarize the information in written minutes of the meeting.

Sample Agenda (first meeting)

1. Open with icebreaker activity.
2. Discuss/define project.
3. Elect officers.
4. Brainstorm ideas and create an Action Plan (see details below).
5. Break for snacks.
6. Set next meeting date, time and place.
7. Clean up.

How to get ideas and keep them organized

Whatever your project, there are probably many ways you and your friends can volunteer time. Finding the best and most agreeable way is best done by group brainstorming.

Once you get everyone at your first meeting and you've had an icebreaker activity, announce that you want to brainstorm to find ways to tackle the project.

Brainstorming is exactly what it sounds like: You storm a large piece of paper or blackboard with ideas. Doing this with the whole group gives everyone a sense of accomplishment and contribution. Before you begin, assign someone the task of recording all the suggestions and go over these rules:

- No idea gets thrown out. Everything goes on the paper, no matter how outrageous.
- Once you've brainstormed for some time, stop and take a look at what you have.
- Narrow your choices. This can be done in small groups, by voting or by consensus of opinion. This is the time when ideas can and should be discarded, until all you're left with are those that your group is willing and able to handle.

Creating an Action Plan

Once you have decided exactly what you want to do, you should create an Action Plan like the one given as an example at the end of this chapter. One of the samples is a blank form that you can copy for your own meeting. The other is an example of how the form was used by a group of teens who wanted to do something about the lack of respect shown by students toward each other. They organized a RESPECT team and planned a number of activities over a six-month period. The plan shows exactly what they wanted to do and how they did it.

This kind of chart helps everyone see the entire picture, keep track of where it's going and remember who's responsible for what. All you need is a large piece of chart paper and some markers. (A blackboard would do, but you'll need someone to copy the information on paper because you can't take the blackboard with you when you go.)

Take a look at the sample plan on pages 122 and 123. You'll see that it keeps track of vital information. At a glance you'll know:

1. What you want to do
2. Who's responsible for doing it
3. How it will be done
4. Where it will be done
5. The resources needed to do it
6. Who's ultimately accountable and when

Looking forward to next time

Once you've set your goals and decided who will be responsible for doing what and by when, decide on your next meeting date. Never leave a meeting (and don't let anyone else leave) without setting up the next meeting. It will save you lots of unnecessary phone calls.

Before your next meeting, you'll need to create an agenda that follows up what happened at your first meeting. The agenda for your next meeting might look something like the one that follows.

Sample Agenda (for following meetings)

1. Open with icebreaker activity.
2. Read minutes from previous meeting.
3. Treasurer gives report.
4. Update on progress: Check Action Plan, listen to committee reports and add new tasks.
5. Break for snacks.
6. Set next meeting date, time and place.
7. Clean up.

Teens in action

Let's take a look at a group of teens who had an idea and made it work.

Teri Nguyen wanted to raise environmental awareness in her community. Knowing she'd need the help of other students to do it, Teri asked her friends at school to join her. Next she found that they could meet only as a school group if they had a faculty sponsor. Easily convinced by Teri's enthusiasm, Mr. Samtak became their sponsor. Then she discovered that to be on the school's list of approved activities, they'd need a constitution and bylaws. Not knowing where to begin, Teri asked existing school groups for help. Using other constitutions as examples, Teri's group soon drafted their own simple constitution that stated their purpose, minimum number of meetings and the function and length of term for each officer.

Now they were an official club and ready to roll. Teri set a meeting date, and when the time came, she and her friends gathered in the school cafeteria.

They decided to begin with small projects like selling T-shirts to raise money and to let people know they existed. They also agreed to join a national affiliation and to contribute some of their money to international environmental groups like Greenpeace. At later meetings, they developed plans to bring awareness projects into the elementary schools in their district.

Over the next four years, the club grew in size and in ambition. They decided they were ready to direct some attention toward environmental problems in their town. “There were barrels dumped into our lake about 50 years ago because the owners didn’t know what else to do with them,” says Teri’s younger sister, An, a former club president. “We wanted to remove them.” An took that idea and ran with it. The cost of removing the barrels was several thousand dollars, but that didn’t stop these volunteers. They organized more T-shirt sales, held a rock concert at the high school and sponsored a 10K local run. Then An applied for a grant from the area conservancy that was approved and matched the funds the volunteers had raised. An, now in college, is proud of her efforts. “It is great,” she says, “that I can come back and find that I left something behind for the town and the club.”

This is just one of many instances where no organization exists to address the needs of a town or school, and so teens step in and take care of it.

What about money?

Is your idea bigger than your budget? Are your members immediately discouraged because they say, “We could never afford that?” Fear not! There are plenty of ways to get money.

One way is to simply ask for the money. One group of volunteers wanted to bring a theater company to school to do a dramatic presentation and discussion about date rape. The volunteers raised more than $1,000 in three weeks by sending letters to area merchants and organizations and then following up with well-researched and well-rehearsed telephone and personal contacts. Sometimes organizations need charitable ways to spend some money; you never know when you may hit the right button at the right time.

Another group discovered the art of grant writing. The government has grant money for all kinds of programs. All you need is the perseverance to work through the application. Get your advisor or another adult to help you. For more information about grants, contact your local Municipal Alliance Committee or your high school principal.

Don't overlook local organizations like the Rotary, Lions Club, chambers of commerce and other groups that make donations to worthwhile causes. Again, your faculty advisor or another supportive adult can help you find these groups. But be prepared to do the legwork yourself. Talk to people, write to them, and talk to them again. Don't be afraid to be persistent; the worst that can happen is that they'll say "no." Meanwhile, you've gained experience, established a possible future contact and gained exposure for your project.

When you ask for money, make it sound sincere and official. On page 124 you'll find a sample letter that you can use as is or can change to meet your needs. (Note: You should use stationery with official-looking letterhead. Ask your school if you can use theirs or design your own.)

There are also awards that you or your group may apply for. Once you've started your project, check into possibilities like SADD's Awareness Contest or the Do Something! grant program. Information about these programs is in the Directory. Your guidance counselor should also have information about programs like these.

Another idea

The opportunities for starting a grassroots volunteer program are endless. Here's one example of a program initiated by teens:

In one city, a group of students decided to fill a long, boring summer with puppet shows for young children. Once they made the decision to start a puppet troupe, they looked for sources of financial support. Their local librarian contacted the Friends of the Library, and the group offered to buy the puppet stage. This was the most expensive item on their list, so they knew they could do the rest themselves. They collected puppets from garage sales, elementary and day-care teachers and thrift shops. Some artistically talented students even made puppets themselves.

Next they were ready to look for more volunteers. The librarian again helped by distributing applications. These forms outlined the project and specified the number of hours involved and the rehearsal dates and times. This helped to minimize the number of volunteers who might drop out and disrupt the schedule of the performances.

Finally, it was time to do it. A meeting date was set and an agenda planned. At this first gathering there were lots of willing volunteers, and the idea looked like it could become a reality. Ground rules were established; attendance and punctuality were stressed. Then a schedule was set. Planning meetings, construction sessions and rehearsals were soon under way. A successful summer of six performances, each before 250 to 300 children, followed.

Starting a puppet troupe like this is a terrific way to have some creative fun and entertain kids as well. But it's also the kind of project that needs an enthusiastic and determined teenager to get it going. If you like the idea, you can get more information from Jean J. Speight of the Castlewood Public Library, 6739 S. Uinta, Englewood, CO 80112.

Get going

From puppet performances to cleaning up ponds, the possibilities are endless. You already have what it takes—the heart to care about something and the energy to do something about it. Take the ideas from this chapter, expand them, modify them, cut out what you don't need and then—*go!* And good luck.

COMMUNITY Anytown, USA

PROJECT NAME R-E-S-P-E-C-T

ACTION PLAN

Tiers	What is to be accomplished? (Steps)	Who is responsible? (Key Person)	How is it to be accomplished?	When is it to be accomplished?	Resources Needed Supplies Materials Logistics	Accountability What is to be reported to whom and by when?
Initial meeting	Organization Set up meeting sched.	everyone, Sue	discussion send list to all members	Feb 15 by Feb 22	meeting room paper, stamps?	Jan – by 2/23
Mini-projects	① Positive quote poster	Edie, Lisa	Print posters, get permission to hang posters	March 30	Books of quotes Songs, poems paper supplies, tape	Ed - by 3/25
	② Dress up day	Linda, Ken	have kids and teachers dress up for 1 day; offer prizes, incentives	April 30	signs, prizes, explanations, instructions	Maryanne by 4/25
	③ No-insult day	MaryAnne, Ed	Contacting students and staff in advance	May 30	signs/posters	Edie, Lisa by 5/25
	④ Positive t-shirt day	Jan, Sue	contacting students and staff in advance	June 15	signs/posters	Ed, Ken by 6/10
Final activity	Recognition breakfast	everyone	students/teachers nominate others for special acts of kindness/compassion	Nov. 25	cafeteria, food decorations, paper supplies	Jan, Sue by Nov. 1
Evaluation	Assessment of projects	Ed	written reaction sheet	Nov. 30	paper, printing	Ken, Edie by 11/20

SCHOOL DISTRICT ______________________________

SCHOOL TEAM NAME ______________________________

ACTION PLAN

Tiers	What is to be accomplished? (Steps)	Who is responsible? (Key Person)	How is it to be accomplished?	When is it to be accomplished?	Resources Needed Supplies Materials Logistics	Accountability What is to be reported to whom and by when?

Sample letter asking for financial help

Date

Company Name
Street Address
Town, State Zip

Dear ______________,

I am a member of the ____________ program. We are a group concerned about __________________. We are working to bring about a positive change by [explain your project here].

Our project will cost about _________ to complete. So far, we've been able to raise _______, but now we need help. We are writing to concerned individuals like you to ask for donations for work. Even a small amount will help. If you have any questions about the group or our project, we would be happy to answer them.

If you'd like to contribute, please make your check payable to

_______________.

Thank you for your attention and your concern.

Sincerely,

[your full name]

Epilogue

So there you have it—a sampling of the many ways teenagers all over America are volunteering their time and energy to worthwhile causes. Their efforts make this country we live in a kinder, safer and healthier place.

And more good news: Studies have shown that people who volunteer in their teens are likely to continue volunteer work into adulthood, maintaining the volunteer backbone of this country.

In fact, if you find that you enjoy community service, you might want to take your work one step further when you graduate high school by serving in a program called AmeriCorps. This is a government program created when President Clinton signed the National and Community Service Act of 1993. AmeriCorps is a pool of 20,000 young people committed to addressing the nation's critical education, human, public safety and environmental needs at the community level—and to paying tuition bills at the same time.

Citizens and legal resident aliens aged 17 years or older (16 for programs targeted to out-of-school youths) may serve in AmeriCorps before, during or after post-secondary education.

Participants are paid during their term of service. For one year of full-time or two years of part-time service, participants receive $4,725 as an education award and for repayment of interest on student loans during their service. This money can also be used to pay for higher education or for vocational training. Full-time participants not otherwise covered receive basic health insurance and may receive a child-care allowance if they need it to participate.

AmeriCorps requires an intense commitment of hours. Participants can perform a 1,700-hour, full-time term for a period of nine months to a year, or a part-time term of 900 hours for one to two years (one to three years for full-time college students). There are a few thousand summer positions also available.

AmeriCorps members work to improve communities in a variety of ways. You may serve alongside experts studying or working on the conservation of cultural and natural resources. You might work one-on-one with children in child-care centers. Or you might assist people with disabilities, people with AIDS or seniors living on their own. You could find yourself renovating and repairing low-income housing. Or you might work to make communities safer by assisting in programs that teach conflict resolution skills to young teens or working with activity centers that offer kids a safe and supervised place to go.

As you can see, AmeriCorps is an extension of the volunteer efforts millions of teens have already begun. Now your commitment to helping America may also help you pay college tuition.

If you want information about AmeriCorps, write or call the headquarters listed in the Directory. In the meantime, if you have a volunteer story you'd like to share, I'd love to hear from you. I know I've only scratched the surface of the outstanding volunteer efforts going on every day all over America. You can write to me at:

Theresa DiGeronimo
c/o Career Press
3 Tice Road
P.O. Box 687
Franklin Lakes, NJ 07417

Directory

Resources by Chapter

Chapter Two: Health Care

American Hospital Association (AHA)
Division of Volunteer Services
1 N. Franklin, Ste. 27
Chicago, IL 60606
312-422-3000

The American Hospital Association can refer you to hospitals in your area that have a junior volunteer program.

American Red Cross (ARC)
National Headquarters
430 17th St. NW
Washington, DC 20006
202-737-8300

For a description, see ARC in the Chapter Four directory listings.

Arthritis Foundation (AF)
P.O. Box 19000
Atlanta, GA 30326
800-283-7800

There are more than 70 AF chapters nationwide serving the needs of people with arthritis. AF relies on volunteers and looks to teens to do administrative support work such as typing, photocopying and addressing envelopes. You can find your nearest AF chapter by looking in your phone directory or by calling their 800 phone number.

March of Dimes Birth Defects Foundation
National Office
1275 Mamaroneck Ave.
White Plains, NY 10605
914-428-7100

The March of Dimes works to prevent birth defects and infant mortality. There are more than 350 offices throughout the country and all welcome teen volunteers. The most popular event is their annual Walk-America fund raiser which relies on volunteers from December through April in more than 1,200 communities. Volunteers are needed to prepare, set up, staff checkpoints, serve refreshments and, of course, walk to raise funds. Also, any individual, school or religious group can volunteer at the local March of Dimes to help with their many ongoing projects. Call your local March of Dimes office, listed in the white pages of the phone book.

National Multiple Sclerosis Society (NMSS)
733 3rd Ave.
New York, NY 10017
212-986-3240

Multiple sclerosis is a chronic disease of the central nervous system that affects people in their 20s or 30s. Teen volunteers are needed to participate in the various fund-raising activities sponsored by the society on both the national and local level. MSS activities include a walk-a-thon, phone-a-thon, bike-a-thon, bowl-a-thon and even a karate kick-a-thon. Call the national headquarters in New York to find the MSS office in your area.

Prevent Blindness America
500 E. Remington Rd.
Schaumburg, IL 60173
800-331-2020

Prevent Blindness America is a national organization dedicated to ending blindness in America. Its network of state affiliates has 40,000 members. Volunteers help with membership drives, fund raising and community support groups. Call the 800 number for the location of the affiliate nearest you.

The Arc of the United States
National Headquarters
500 E. Border St., Ste. 300
Arlington, TX 76010
817-261-6003

The Arc is a national organization concerned with mental disabilities. Through advocacy, education, job training and placement, the Arc helps mentally retarded people live, work and play. The Arc has a quarter of a million members in independent chapters across the country. Each chapter varies in its volunteer opportunities, depending on its size, budget and the needs of the local community. Write to the national headquarters in Arlington, Texas, to find the chapter nearest you.

Chapter Three: Substance Abuse Prevention

Just Say No International
2101 Webster St., Ste. 1300
Oakland, CA 94612
800-258-2766

Just Say No offers three projects for teens called "Transitions," "Peer Tutoring" and "CommUnity Service." In addition to addressing drug issues, these programs emphasize resistance skills. Find out about these projects by calling the international headquarters.

Mothers Against Drunk Driving (MADD)
P.O. Box 541688
Dallas, TX 75354
800-GET-MADD

National Clearinghouse for Alcohol and Drug Information (NCADI)
P.O. Box 2345
Rockville, MD 20847
800-729-6686

This organization is primarily a source of information about alcohol and other drugs. It is a service of the Office for Substance Abuse Prevention of the U.S. Department of Health and Human Services. Through NCADI you can obtain a listing of organizations in your area dedicated to substance abuse prevention. You can also request free materials on substance abuse education and prevention. Call the 800 number for a catalog.

National Council on Alcoholism and Drug Dependence (NCADD)
12 W. 21st St.
New York, NY 10010
800-622-2255

NCADD is dedicated to educating the public about alcoholism and drug addiction as treatable and preventable diseases. It has affiliates in 36 states and Washington, D.C. Opportunities for teen volunteers vary. Most affiliates use volunteers to help answer phones, do office work and mail information to the public. Call the national headquarters to find the local office nearest you.

Remove Intoxicated Drivers (RID)
P.O. Box 520
Schenectady, NY 12301
518-372-0034

If your community does not have a RID chapter, contact the Schenectady, New York office for information on the location of the nearest chapter or on starting your own chapter.

Students Against Driving Drunk (SADD)
P.O. Box 800
Marlboro, MA 01752
508-481-3568

The goals of SADD are the elimination of underage drinking, drugging and driving under the influence. Members have saved thousands of lives with education, peer counseling programs and community awareness projects. SADD supports sober driver programs in the effort to stop teen drinking and driving. If you are interested in starting a SADD chapter in your school, contact the headquarters and request "How to Start Your SADD Chapter and New Ideas for Existing SADD Chapters."

Chapter Four: The Needy

American Red Cross (ARC)
National Headquarters
430 17th St. NW
Washington, DC 20006
202-737-8300

The American Red Cross (ARC) provides relief to victims of disasters and helps people prevent, prepare for and respond to emergencies. ARC also sponsors programs and activities for and by teenagers. ARC has 2,700 chapters throughout the U.S. and its territories, as well as field stations on U.S. military installations. Approximately 16 percent of ARC's 1.5 million volunteers are under 18. Some chapters have youth volunteer programs, and others use teens alongside adult volunteers. Check your phone book for the ARC nearest you.

CARE
151 Ellis St.
Atlanta, GA 30303
404-681-2552

CARE is a worldwide organization dedicated to serving the poor in more than 35 countries. In its regional offices, volunteers help with clerical tasks, participate in public fund raising and awareness events and collect food and medical supplies for disaster relief. Your high school service club can establish a relationship with CARE to provide volunteers immediately after a disaster has occurred. Call the number above for the location of the chapter nearest you.

Christmas in April USA
1225 Eye St. NW, Ste. 601
Washington, DC 20005
202-326-8268

On the last Saturday in April (and on other days as well) CIA volunteers across the country rebuild thousands of homes with donated building materials. While skilled tradesman and professionals are needed for most of the physical work, teens can volunteer in support capacities. Contact the director at the national headquarters to find out if there is a program in your area.

Food for the Hungry
P.O. Box 12349
Scottsdale, AZ 85267
800-2-HUNGER

This organization uses more than 150,000 volunteers to collect food, raise funds and publicize their efforts. As a Christian organization, much of its local work is done through church groups. Contact the organization to find a church group near you or to find out how your church can become a Food for the Hungry supporter.

The Gleaning Network
Society of St. Andrew
P.O. Box 329
State Route 615
Big Island, VA 24526
804-333-4597
Contact: Director of Gleaning Ministries

Gleaners are mentioned several times in the Bible as people who go into fields and orchards to pick the vegetables and fruits that remain after harvest. Gleaners share this produce with those in need.

Because most farmers find it too labor-intensive and uneconomical to pick the food after the regular harvest is done, 20 percent of food produced for human consumption in the United States is lost—more than 135 million tons worth more than $30 billion. The Gleaning Network has groups in Virginia, Pennsylvania, North Carolina, South Carolina, Maryland and Washington, D.C. Gleaning groups come from churches, neighborhoods, Scout troops, senior groups and other organizations and can number from five to 250 people. Gleaners should be able to bend over and lift about 20 pounds of produce. For information about volunteering, call the national headquarters.

Habitat for Humanity International
121 Habitat St.
Americus, GA 31709
912-924-6935

All of Habitat's 700-plus affiliates are staffed by volunteers. There are 23 established high school chapters and 307 college chapters. In some states, teens are involved in the planning and construction of new homes. In all chapters, teens are needed for clerical work, fund raising and supply collections. Contact the national office listed to find the Habitat for Humanity office nearest you.

National Coalition for the Homeless
1612 K St., NW, #1004
Washington, DC 20006
202-775-1322

If you are interested in finding out about what people are doing to fight homelessness in your area, the National Coalition for the Homeless can provide that information.

National Student Campaign Against Hunger and Homelessness (NSCAHH)
29 Temple Place
Boston, MA 02111
617-292-4823

The National Student Campaign Against Hunger and Homelessness has more than 450 afflilates in schools nationwide. Its goal is to provide students and educators with the resources, ideas and motivation to fight hunger and homelessness in every interested community. Among its national programs are National Hunger and Homeless Week, the Hunger Clean-up and the Food Salvage Program. While these are annual activities, NSCAHH volunteers work year-round in service to their communities.

Reading Is Fundamental
Smithsonian Institute
600 Maryland Ave. SW, Ste. 600
Washington, DC 20024
202-287-3220

See Reading Is Fundamental in the Chapter Five directory listings for complete details.

Second Harvest
343 S. Dearborn
Chicago, IL 60604
312-341-1303

Second Harvest is a national network of food banks that provides food for organizations dedicated to feeding the hungry. Each local food bank is independently run and funded. Volunteers can help with clerical and warehouse work. The national headquarters office will tell you where there is a food bank near you.

Chapter Five: Education

American Library Association
Coalition for Literacy
50 E. Huron St.
Chicago, IL 60611
312-944-6780

The American Library Association promotes library services. They are affiliated with Literacy Volunteers of America, Laubach Literacy International and Laubach Literacy Action.

American Literacy Council
454 Riverside Dr.
New York, NY 10027
212-662-0650

The American Literacy Council strives to improve literacy through the use of computer techniques. The Council sponsors the SoundSpeller remedial computer-tutor program for adolescents and adults.

Book It! Pizza Hut, Inc.
P.O. Box 2999
Wichita, KS 67201
800-4-Book-It

Book It! is a five-month national reading incentive program for kids in kindergarten through sixth grade. It runs from October to February each year. Teachers set monthly reading goals for students, and when they reach that goal, each student receives a certificate for a free Personal Pan Pizza from Pizza Hut. At the end of the period, if the entire class has met the goal four of the five months, the class receives a pizza party. Teens from middle or high school can set up and monitor the program!

Business Council for Effective Literacy
1221 Ave. of the Americas, 35th Fl.
New York, NY 10020
212-512-2415

The Business Council for Effective Literacy is a publicly supported foundation dedicated to advancing adult literacy in the U.S.

Christian Literacy Center
541 Perry Highway
Pittsburgh, PA 15229
412-364-3777

The Christian Literacy Center is comprised of Christian professionals and paraprofessionals who prepare basic adult literacy materials for use through churches. Volunteers are needed to do clerical work, train tutors and plan literacy projects.

Contact Literacy Center
800-228-8813

This hotline number can be used to find literacy programs near you.

Future Educators of America
c/o Phi Delta Kappa International
P.O. Box 789
Bloomington, IN 47402
800-766-1156

Phi Delta Kappa, the professional fraternity in education, organizes Future Educators of America clubs in middle and high schools across the United States. Members of these clubs get hands-on teaching experience by volunteering to tutor. If you'd like more information about these clubs or would like to start one in your own school, call the toll-free number.

Laubach Literacy International
1320 Jamesville Ave.
Syracuse, NY 13210
315-422-9121

Laubach Literacy International trains tutors for individual and small-group teaching of adults with low or no English-language reading skills, trains and coordinates leaders for local groups, educates the public about literacy programs, and publishes materials for new adult readers. Laubach primarily uses adults as tutors, although some Laubach materials may be used in peer-group projects. Older teens can serve as tutors, and volunteers of all ages can help with distributing information and providing backup services.

Literacy Volunteers of America
5795 Widewaters Parkway
Syracuse, NY 13214
315-445-8000

The Literacy Volunteers of America train and aid individuals and organizations seeking to tutor adults in basic literacy and conversational English.

Reading Is Fundamental
Smithsonian Institute
600 Maryland Ave. SW, Ste. 600
Washington, DC 20024
202-287-3220

Reading is Fundamental works through a nationwide network of 5,000 community-based projects that promote reading among young people. These projects are run by volunteers who motivate youngsters to want to read by letting them choose and keep books they like and by showing them that reading is fun and important.

Chapter Six: Protecting the Environment

American Forests
Global Releaf Program
P.O. Box 2000
Washington, DC 20013
202-667-3300

This association can help you establish a tree-planting program.

Center for Marine Conservation
1725 DeSales St. NW
Washington, DC 20036
202-429-5609

Every year in September, the Center for Marine Conservation sponsors a nationwide, three-hour beach cleanup. Call them for the group nearest you.

Clean Water Action
1320 18th St. NW, Ste. 300
Washington, DC 20036
202-457-1286

This is a national citizens' organization that relies on education, grassroots organizing and lobbying to influence public policy decisions for clean and safe water at an affordable cost.

Greenpeace USA, Inc.
1436 U St. NW
Washington, DC 20009
202-462-1177

Greenpeace USA is a nonprofit group fighting for the preservation of endangered species and the environment and dedicated to the prevention of nuclear war.

The Izaak Walton League of America
707 Conservation Lane
Gaithersburg, MD 20878
301-548-0150

The Izaak Walton League of America is a national nonprofit conservation organization formed in 1922 and is dedicated to protection of America's soil, air, woods, water and wildlife. The league is made up of 54,000 members in 400 local chapters nationwide. The league sponsors a program called Save Our Streams (SOS). SOS asks volunteers to monitor, protect and restore America's waters through simple, fun, hands-on techniques.

Keep America Beautiful, Inc.
Mill River Plaza
9 W. Broad St.
Stamford, CT 06902
203-323-8987

Keep America Beautiful, Inc. (KAB) is a national, nonprofit public education organization dedicated to improving waste handling practices in American communities. More than 485 cities, towns and counties in 41 states are implementing the KAB System with great success. Litter reductions of up to 80 percent have been sustained in many KAB System communities. Changing attitudes and behaviors is a lasting solution and not simply a one-time cleanup. Call the national office to find out how your community can join the KAB System.

Kids Against Pollution (KAP)
P.O Box 775
Closter, NJ 07624
201-784-0726

Kids Against Pollution has 500 chapters organized in 42 states. You can write to them for a packet of information on environmental issues, suggestions for action and a copy of a constitutional amendment that is waiting to be passed at both the state and federal levels.

National Arbor Day Foundation
100 Arbor Ave.
Nebraska City, NE 68410
402-979-3000

Members receive inexpensive seedlings, information on tree planting, posters and educational materials.

National Audubon Society
700 Broadway
New York, NY 10003
212-797-3000

This is a membership group that uses policy research, scientific study, lobbying, litigation, citizen action and education to protect natural habitats and resources.

National Park Service
(U.S. Department of Interior)
P.O. Box 37127
Washington, DC 20013
202-208-6843

The National Park Service administers parks, monuments and other nationally significant sites and coordinates the Wild and Scenic Rivers System and the National Trail System.

National Wildlife Federation
1400 16th St. NW
Washington, DC 20036
202-797-6800

This citizen's organization is dedicated to assisting and inspiring individuals and organizations to conserving wild species, habitats and natural resources, and to protecting the earth's environment.

The Nature Conservancy
1815 N. Lynn St.
Arlington, VA 22209
703-841-5300

This nonprofit membership group works for the preservation of biological diversity by protecting natural habitats, leading state natural heritage programs and managing a system of more than 1,600 U.S. nature sanctuaries.

Sierra Club
730 Polk St.
San Francisco, CA 94109
415-776-2211

Sierra Club members are involved in legislation, litigation, public information, publishing, wilderness outings and conferences aimed at enjoying and protecting the earth's wild places and natural resources.

Student Conservation Association, Inc.
SCA High School Program
P.O. Box 550
Charleston, NH 03603
603-543-1700

The Student Conservation Association has developed a unique program where students participate in outdoor work projects.

Student Environmental Action Coalition (SEAC)
National Office
P.O. Box 1168
Chapel Hill, NC 27514
919-967-4600

SEAC is a grassroots coalition of student and youth enviromental groups in more than 2,000 high schools in all 50 states. SEAC can help with local campaigns and issues or put you in touch with other activists. Call the headquarters to get in touch with your regional or state coordinating group.

Water Pollution Control Federation
Public Education Department
601 Wythe St.
Alexandria, VA 22314
703-684-2400

The Federation will supply information on water conservation such as "Wastewater Treatment: The Student's Resource Guide."

The Wilderness Society
900 17th St. NW
Washington, DC 20006
202-833-2300

The Wilderness Society is a nonprofit membership group dedicated to preserving wilderness and wildlife and promoting an American land ethic.

Chapter Seven: Politics

Teenage Republicans (TAR)
National TAR Headquarters
P.O. Box 1896
10620-C Crestwood Dr.
Manassas, VA 22110
703-368-4214

Young Democrats of America
Democratic National Committee
430 S. Capitol St. SE
Washington, DC 20003
202-863-8000

Chapter Eight: Doing It Yourself

Do Something!
1 World Trade Center, 78th Fl.
New York, NY 10048

Do Something! is a national nonprofit organization founded and managed by young people seeking to inspire and assist other young people to take action in their communities. If you have a creative solution to a problem in your community, you can apply for a Do Something! National Grant for up to $500 by writing: Do Something! National Grants, P.O. Box 2409 JAF, New York, NY 10116. You can become a Do Something! member by calling 1-900-ALL OF US. Members receive a membership card, newsletter and updates on the progress of Do Something!, as well as other ideas about how you can get involved in community change. A membership fee of $10 will be charged to your phone bill when you call.

Key Club, Inc.
3636 Woodview Trace
Indianapolis, IN 46268
317-875-8755

Key Clubs are sponsored by Kiwanis Clubs. Kiwanis is a worldwide service organization whose members have the desire to become personally involved in making their communities better places in which to live. Key Clubs are for teenagers who want to work together to fulfill the needs of their schools and communities through volunteer service. Call the national office to find a Kiwanis Club that can sponsor your volunteer project. They can offer guidance, supervision, ideas and funds.

Youth Service America
1101 15th St. NW, Ste. 200
Washington, DC 20005
202-296-2992

National Youth Service: Answer the Call, A Resource Guide is a publication of Youth Service America that profiles more than 50 youth service programs and 80 national and community organizations. It also highlights funding, technical assistance and training resources, lists youth service award programs and offers a bibliography of more than 200 publications.

Epilogue

AmeriCorps
1100 Vermont Ave. NW
Washington, DC 20525
800-94-ACORPS

National Volunteer Centers

Alabama

State of Alabama
Governor's Office on
Volunteerism
600 Dexter Ave.
Montgomery, AL 36130
205-242-4511

Alabama National &
Community Service State
Commission
600 Dexter Ave., Rm. SB 06
Montgomery, AL 36130
334-242-7110

United Way Volunteer Center
1505 Wilmer Ave.
P.O. Box 1122
Anniston, AL 36202
205-236-8229

United Way Volunteer Center
3600 8th Ave. S., Ste. 504
Birmingham, AL 35222
205-251-5131

The Volunteer Center
of Morgan County
1403 Office Park W., Ste. G
Decatur, AL 35603
205-355-8628

Volunteer Action of
the Eastern Shore
150 S. Greeno Rd., Ste. P
P.O. Box 61
Fairhope, AL 36533
205-928-0509

Volunteer Center of
Huntsville/Madison Counties
1101 Washington St.
P.O. Box 18094
Huntsville, AL 35804
205-539-7797

Volunteer Mobile, Inc.
2504 Dauphin St., Ste. K
Mobile, AL 36606
205-479-0631

VAC/Information & Referral, Inc.
2125 E. South Blvd.
P.O. Box 11044
Montgomery, AL 36111
205-284-0006

Alaska

Alaska State Community
Service Commission
333 W. 4th Ave., Ste. 222
Anchorage, AK 99501
907-269-4611

UW of Anchorage/
Volunteer Center
341 W. Tudor Rd., Ste. 106
Anchorage, AK 99503
907-562-4483

Voluntary Action Center of UW
P.O. Box 74396
Fairbanks, AK 99707
907-452-7000

Arizona

Arizona National & Community
Service State Commission
1700 W. Washington St.
3rd Floor, Rm. 320
Phoenix, AZ 85007
602-542-3461

Volunteer Center
of Maricopa County
1515 E. Osborn
Phoenix, AZ 85014
602-263-9736

Volunteer Center
of Yavapai County
107 N. Cortez, Rm. 208
Prescott, AZ 86301
602-776-9908

Volunteer Center
6840 E. Broadway
Tucson, AZ 85710
602-886-6500

Arkansas

State of Arkansas
Arkansas Division
of Volunteerism
P.O. Box 1437 Slot #1300
Little Rock, AR 72203
501-682-7540

Arkansas National &
Community Service State
Commission
Donaghey Plaza S.,
7th & Main, Ste. 1300
Little Rock, AR 72201
501-682-6214

United Way VAC
700 W. Capitol, Rm. 2506
Little Rock, AR 72201
501-324-5234

California

California Commission on
Improving Life Through Service
1121 L St., Ste. 600
Sacramento, CA 95814
916-323-7646

Volunteer Center
of Placer County
DeWitt Center
11566 O Ave.
Auburn, CA 85603
916-885-7706

Volunteer Center of Kern County
601 Chester Ave.
Bakersfield, CA 93301
805-327-9346

Volunteer Center
of Santa Cruz County
P.O. Box 93
Ben Lomond, CA 95005
408-336-2257

Community Action Volunteers
in Education
W. 2nd & Cherry Streets
Chico, CA 95929
916-898-5817

Volunteer Center of Contra
Costa County
1070 Concord Ave., Ste. 100
Concord, CA 94520
415-246-1050

Downey Volunteer Center
11026 Downey Ave.
Downey, CA 90241
310-881-1712

Volunteer Center
of the Redwoods
3300 Glenwood St.
Eureka, CA 95501
707-442-3711

Volunteer Center
of Solano County
744 Empire St., Ste. 204
Fairfield, CA 94533
707-427-6699

The Volunteer Bureau of
Fresno County, Inc.
1900 Mariposa Mall, Ste. 303
Fresno, CA 93721
209-237-3101

VAC of Nevada County
10139 Joerschke Dr.
Grass Valley, CA 95945
916-272-5041

Hayward Volunteer Center
21455 Birch St.
Hayward, CA 94541
514-538-0554

Volunteer Center Orange
County West
16168 Beach Blvd., Ste. 121
Huntington Beach, CA 92647
714-375-7751

La Mirada Volunteer Center
12900 Bluefield Ave.
La Mirada, CA 90638
213-484-2849

Volunteer Center Lancaster
Court Office
1040 West Ave., J#127
Lancaster, CA 93535
805-945-6357

Volunteer Center of Los Angeles
2117 W. Temple St., 3rd Fl.
Los Angeles, CA 90026
213-484-2849

Volunteer Center Stanislaus
2937 Veneman Ave.
Modesto, CA 95355
209-524-1307

Monrovia Volunteer Center
119 W. Palm Ave.
Monrovia, CA 91016
818-357-3797

VC of the Monterey Peninsula
801 Lighthouse Ave.
Monterey, CA 93940
408-655-9234

VC of Napa County
1820 Jefferson St.
Napa, CA 94559
707-252-6222

VC of Alamenda County
1212 Broadway, Ste. 506
Oakland, CA 94612
510-893-7147

Volunteer Center
of San Fernando Valley
8134 Van Nuys Blvd. #200
Panorama City, CA 91402
818-908-5066

Volunteer Center
of San Gabriel Valley
3301 Thorndale Rd.
Pasadena, CA 91107
818-792-6118

Volunteers Involved
for Pasadena
234 W. Colorado Blvd., Rm. 205
Pasadena, CA 91101
818-796-6926

Valley Volunteer Center
333 Division St.
Pleasanton, CA 94566
415-462-3570

VC of the Greater
Pomona Valley
436 W. Fourth St., Ste. 201
Pomona, CA 91766
909-629-1187

VC of Riverside
P.O. Box 5376
Riverside, CA 92517
909-686-4402

Voluntary Action Center
P.O. Box 878
S. Lake Tahoe, CA 96156
916-541-2611

VC of Sacramento/
Yolo Counties
8912 Volunteer Lane, Ste. 140
Sacramento, CA 95826
916-368-3110

Volunteer Center
of the Inland Empire
1325 Auto Plaza Dr., Ste. 140B
San Bernardino, CA 92408
909-884-2558

United Way of San Diego
Volunteer Center
P.O. Box 23543
San Diego, CA 92123
619-492-2090

VC of San Francisco
1160 Battery St., Ste. 70
San Francisco, CA 94111
415-982-8999

Volunteerism Project/
United Way
50 California St., Ste. 50
San Francisco, CA 94111
415-772-7393

The Volunteer Exchange of
Santa Clara County
1922 The Alameda, Ste. 211
San Jose, CA 95128
408-247-1126

VC of San Mateo County
800 S. Claremont, Ste. 108
San Mateo, CA 94402
415-342-0801

VC of Marin
770 Skyview Terrace
San Rafael, CA 94903
415-479-5660

VC of Greater Orange County
1000 E. Santa Ana Blvd.,
Ste. 200
Santa Ana, CA 92701
714-953-5757

VC of Santa Cruz County
575 Soquel Ave.
Santa Cruz, CA 95062
408-423-0554

VC of Sonoma County
1041 Fourth St.
Santa Rosa, CA 95404
707-573-3399

VAC of South Lake Tahoe
P.O. Box 878
South Lake Tahoe, CA 95705
916-541-2611

Volunteer Center of UW/
San Joaquin Vally
265 W. Knolls Way
Stockton, CA 95204
209-943-0870

VC South Bay Harbor—
Long Beach
1230 Cravens Ave.
Torrance, CA 90501
310-212-5009

Tulare Volunteer Bureau
115 S. M St.
Tulare, CA 93274
209-688-05539

Volunteer Center
of Mendocino County
505 S. State St.
Ukiah, CA 95482
707-462-8945

Volunteer Center
of Victor Valley
15561 Seventh St.
Victorville, CA 92392
619-245-8592

City of Visalia
Volunteer Services Program
417 N. Locust
Visalia, CA 93277
209-738-3485

Watsonville Volunteer Center
15 Madison, Ste. 202
Watsonville, CA 95076
408-722-6708

Colorado

Community Partnership Office
140 E. 19th Ave., Ste. 100
Denver, CO 80203
303-894-2750

Center of Information
& Volunteer Action
110 E. Hallam St., Ste. 126
Aspen, CO 81611
303-925-7887

Volunteer Connection
of Boulder County
2299 Pearl St., Ste. N
Boulder, CO 80303
303-444-4904

Metro Volunteers
225 E. 16th Ave., Ste. 200
Denver, CO 80203
303-894-0103

Volunteer Resource Bureau of
United Way of Weld County
814 9th St.
P.O. Box 1944
Greeley, CO 80631
303-353-4300

Connecticut

Connecticut National &
Community Service State
Commission
61 Woodland St.
Hartford, CT 06105
203-566-6154

Volunteer Action Center
75 Washington Ave.
Bridgeport, CT 06604
203-334-5106

The Volunteer Bureau
of Greater Danbury
337 Main St.
Danbury, CT 06810
203-797-1154

VAC/United Way
30 Laurel St.
Hartford, CT 06106
203-493-1100

VAC of Greater New Haven, Inc.
70 Audubon St.
New Haven, CT 06510
203-785-1997

VAC of Mid-Fairfield
83 East Ave.
Norwalk, CT 06851
203-852-0850

The VC of S.W. Fairfield County
62 Palmer's Hill Rd.
Stamford, CT 06902
203-348-7714

Delaware

State of Delaware
Office of Volunteerism
P.O. Box 637
Dover, DE 19903
302-739-4456

Delaware National &
Community Service State
Commission
Carvel State Office Building,
4th Floor
820 N. French St.
Wilmington, DE 19801
302-577-6650

District of Columbia

D.C. National & Community
Service State Commission
717 14th St. NW, #900
Washington, DC 20005
202-727-4970

Florida

Florida Governor's Commission
on Community Service
1101 Gulf Breeze Pkwy., Box 188
Gulf Breeze, FL 32561
904-934-4000

Volunteer Services of
Manatee County, Inc.
1701 14th St. W., #2
Bradenton, FL 34205
813-746-7117

The VC of Volusia/
Flagler Counties
W. International Speedway Blvd.
Daytona Beach, FL 32124
904-253-0563

Volunteer Broward
1300 S. Andrews Ave.
P.O. Box 22877
Fort Lauderdale, FL 33335
305-522-6761

UW/Volunteer Center of
Hillsborough
110 E. Oak
Tampa, FL 33602
813-274-0909

VAC of Lee County, Inc.
P.O. Box 061039
Fort Myers, FL 33906
813-433-5301

The VC of Alachua County
2815 NW 13th St., Ste. 302
Gainesville, FL 32609
904-378-2552

Volunteer Jacksonville, Inc.
4049 Woodcock Dr., Ste. 100
Jacksonville, FL 32207
904-398-7777

UW of Central Florida
Volunteer Center
P.O. Box 1357
Highland City, FL 33846
813-648-1535

Dade County's Center
for Voluntarism
One SE 3rd Ave., Ste. 1950
Miami, FL 33101
305-579-2259

Volunteer Service Bureau of
Marion County, Inc.
520 SE Fort King, Ste. C-1
Ocala, FL 34471
904-732-4771

VC of Central Florida
1900 N. Mills Ave., Ste. 1
Orlando, FL 32083
407-896-0945

Volunteer Pensacola/VAC, Inc.
7 N. Coyle St.
Pensacola, FL 32501
904-438-5649

The Volunteer Bureau
of Palm Beach County
P.O. Box 20809
West Palm Beach, FL 33416
407-820-2550

Volunteer Center of Sarasota
1750 17th St., #C-3
Sarasota, FL 34234
813-366-0013

Volunteer Action Center
P.O. Box 13087
St. Petersburg, FL 33733
813-893-1140

United Way Volunteer Center
P.O. Box 362
Stuart, FL 34995
407-220-1717

Volunteer Big Bend
307 E. Seventh Ave.
Tallahassee, FL 32303
904-681-0947

Volunteer Center South
400 Tamiami Trail S., Ste. 230
Venice, FL 34285
813-488-5683

Brevard Volunteer Center
1149 Lake Dr.
Cocoa, FL 32922
407-631-2740

Indian River County VAC
2525 St. Lucie Ave.
Vero Beach, FL 32960
407-778-1223

Nassau County Volunteer Center
22 N. 5th St.
Fernandina Beach, FL 32034
904-261-2771

Georgia

Georgia National & Community Service State Commission
2020 Equitable Building
100 Peachtree St.
Atlanta, GA 30303
404-657-7827

UW/Volunteer Albany
P.O. Box 7
Albany, GA 31702
912-883-6700

United Way of Metropolitan Atlanta's Volunteer Resource Center
100 Edgewood Ave. NE, 3rd Fl.
P.O. Box 2692
Atlanta, GA 30303
404-527-7336

UW of the CSRA
630 Ellis St.
Augusta, GA 30901
706-826-4460

The Volunteer Center
1425 3rd Ave.
P.O. Box 1157
Columbus, GA 31902
706-596-8657

VAC of NW Georgia
305 S. Thornton Ave., Ste. 2
Dalton, GA 30720
706-226-4357

Volunteer Resource Center
P.O. Box 1193
Gainesville, GA 30503
404-535-5445

Volunteer Macon
2484 Ingleside Ave., A101
Macon, GA 31204
912-742-6677

VAC of United Way
428 Bull St.
Savannah, GA 31412
912-651-7700

Hawaii

Hawaii State Commission on National & Community Service
335 Merchant St., Rm. 101
Honolulu, HI 96813
808-586-8675

Statewide Volunteer Services
Office of the Governor
State Capitol
Honolulu, HI 96813

VAC of Oahu
680 Iwilei, Ste. 430
Honolulu, HI 96817
808-536-7234

Idaho

Idaho Commission for National & Community Service
650 W. State St., Rm. 307
Boise, ID 83702
208-334-3843

United Way Community Resources
5420 W. Franklin Rd.
Boise, ID 83705
208-345-4357

Illinois

Lt. Governor's Advisory Council on Voluntary Action
James R. Thompson Center
100 W. Randolph, Ste. 15-200
Chicago, IL 60601
312-814-5220

United Way Crusade of Mercy
560 W. Lake St.
Chicago, IL 60661
312-906-2425

Volunteer Center of Knox County
140 E. Main St.
Galesburg, IL 61401
309-343-4434

The Volunteer Center for Lake County
United Way of Lake County
2020 O'Plaine Rd.
Green Oaks, IL 60048
708-816-0063

Volunteer Center of the Greater Quad Cities
1417 6th Ave.
Moline, IL 61265
309-764-6804

Volunteer Center of United Way (of Champaign County)
404 W. Church
Champaign, IL 61820
217-352-5151

Community Volunteer Center
Lincoln Land Community College
Shepherd Rd.
Springfield, IL 62794
217-786-2289

Voluntary Action Center
1606 Bethany Rd.
Sycamore, IL 60178
815-758-3932

Indiana

Governor's Voluntary Action Program
302 W. Washington, Rm. E220
Indianapolis, IN 46204
317-232-2504

First Call for Help/ Volunteer Services
522 Franklin
Columbus, IN 47201
812-376-0011

United Way VAC
101 NW First St., Ste. 215
Evansville, IN 47701
812-421-2801

Volunteer Connection
227 E. Washington Blvd.,
Ste. 202B
Fort Wayne, IN 46802
219-420-4263

The Window Community
Volunteer Center
223 S. Main
Goshen, IN 46526
219-533-9680

The Human Resources
Department of United Way
221 W. Ridge Rd.
Griffith, IN 46319
219-923-2302

Volunteer Action Center
United Way of Central Indiana
3901 N. Meridian St.
P.O. Box 88409
Indianapolis, IN 46208
317-923-1466

Greater Lafayette Volunteer
Bureau
301 1/2 Columbia St.
Lafayette, IN 47901
317-742-8241

Community Resource Center
914 Lincolnway W.
South Bend, IN 46616
219-232-2522

Volunteer Action Center
721 Wabash Ave., Ste. 502
Terre Haute, IN 48707
812-232-8822

Iowa

Governor's Office for Volunteers
State Capitol
Des Moines, IA 50319
1-515-281-8304

Iowa Commission for National
& Community Service
150 E. Des Moines St.
Des Moines, IA 50319
515-281-9043

Voluntary Center of Story County
510 5th St.
Ames, IA 50010
515-232-2736

The Volunteer Bureau of
Council Bluffs
523 6th Ave.
Council Bluffs, IA 51503
712-322-6431

United Way of Central Iowa
Volunteer Center
1111 9th St., Ste. 300
Des Moines, IA 50314
515-246-6545

Johnson County VAC
c/o United Way
911 N. Governor
Iowa City, IA 52240
319-338-7823

The Voluntary Action Center
of Muscatine
113 Iowa Ave.
Muscatine, IA 52761
319-263-0959

VAC of the
Iowa Great Lakes, Inc.
1713 Hill Ave.
Spirit Lake, IA 51360
712-336-4444

The Volunteer Bureau
Cedar Valley United Way
3420 University Ave., Ste. C
Waterloo, IA 50701
319-235-6211

Kansas

Kansas Commission for
National & Community Service
200 SW 6th
P.O. Box 889
Topeka, KS 66603
913-234-1423

Wyandotte County
Volunteer Center
434 Minnesota Ave.
P.O. Box 17-1042
Kansas City, KS 66117
913-371-3674

Roger Hill Volunteer Center
211 E. 8th, Ste. G
P.O. Box 116
Lawrence, KS 66044
913-865-5030

Volunteer Center of Topeka
4125 Gage Center Dr.
Topeka, KS 66604
913-272-8890

United Way Volunteer Center
212 N. Market St., Ste. 200
Wichita, KS 67202
316-267-1321

Kentucky

Kentucky Office
of Volunteer Services
275 E. Main St.
Frankfort, KY 40621
1-502-564-HELP

Kentucky Community Service
Commission
State Office Bldg.
501 Mero St., Rm. 923
Frankfort, KY 40622
502-564-5330

Volunteer and Information
Center, Inc.
236 N. Elm St.
P.O. Box 2009
Henderson, KY 42420
502-831-2273

Volunteer Center
of the Bluegrass
2029 Bellefonte Dr.
Lexington, KY 40503
606-278-6258

The Volunteer Connection
334 E. Broadway
P.O. Box 4488
Louisville, KY 40204
502-266-6328

The Volunteer Center
920 Frederica St., Ste. 1010
P.O. Box 517
Owensboro, KY 42302
502-683-9161

Louisiana

Louisiana Serve Commission
900 N. 3rd St.
Old Pentagon Barracks, Bldg. C
Baton Rouge, LA 70809
504-342-2038

Volunteer Baton Rouge!
4962 Florida Blvd., Ste. 412
Baton Rouge, LA 70806
504-927-8270

Volunteer Center of Lafayette
P.O. Box 52074
Lafayette, LA 70505
318-233-1006

Volunteer Center of SW
Louisiana, Inc.
1023 Common St.
Lake Charles, LA 70601
318-439-6109

United Way of NE
Louisiana, Inc.
1300 Hudson Lane, Ste. 7
Monroe, LA 71201
318-325-3869

Volunteer & Information
Agency, Inc.
4747 Earhart Blvd., Ste. 111
New Orleans, LA 70125
504-488-4636

Maine

Maine Commission on National
& Community Service
State House
184 State St.
Augusta, ME 04333
207-624-6041

Maine Volunteer Connection
P.O. Box 1442
Rockland, ME 04841
207-594-2636 or 207-273-3018

Volunteer! York County
36 Water St., Unit C
Kennebunk, ME 04043
207-985-6869

United Way's Volunteer Center
233 Oxford St.
Portland, ME 04104
207-874-1015

Maryland

Governor's Office
on Volunteerism
301 W. Preston St., Ste. 1501
Baltimore, MD 21201
410-225-4496

Volunteer Center
of Frederick County
22 S. Market St.
Frederick, MD 21701
301-663-9096

Prince Georges Voluntary
Action Center
P.O. Box 187
Hyattsville, MD 20781
301-699-2800

Montgomery County
Volunteer Center
401 Fleet St., Rm. 106
Rockville, MD 20850
301-217-4949

Massachusetts

Massachusetts Commission for
National & Community Service
87 Summer St., 4th Floor
Boston, MA 02110
617-542-2544

VAC/United Way
of Massachusetts Bay
2 Liberty Square
Boston, MA 02109
617-482-8370

VAC/United Way
of Pioneer Valley
184 Mill St.
P.O. Box 3040
Springfield, MA 01102
413-737-2691

United Way of Greater
Attleboro/Taunton, Inc.
P.O. Box 416
Taunton, MA 02703
508-824-3985

Volunteer Resources Division
United Way of Central
Massachusetts
484 Main St., Ste. 300
Worcester, MA 01608
508-757-5631

Michigan

Michigan Community Service
Commission
111 S. Capitol Ave.
Olds Plaza Building, 4th Fl.
Lansing, MI 48909
517-335-4295

The Volunteer Center of Michigan
c/o Michigan Nonprofit Forum
38 Kellogg Center
E. Lansing, MI 48824
517-353-9277

Alpena Volunteer Center
Alpena Community College
666 Johnson St.
Alpena, MI 49707
517-356-9021 ext. 335

Washenaw United Way
Volunteer Action Center
2301 Platt Rd.
P.O. Box 3813
Ann Arbor, MI 48106
313-971-5852

Volunteer Bureau of
Battle Creek, Inc.
182 W. Van Buren St.
Battle Creek, MI 49017
616-965-0555

Volunteer Action Center
of Bay County
315 14th St.
Bay City, MI 48708
517-893-6060

UCS of Metro Detroit
1212 Griswold
Detroit, MI 48226
313-226-9429

United Way of Genesee &
Lapeer Counties
202 E. Boulevard Dr.
Flint, MI 48503
810-767-0500

Volunteer Connection
500 Commerce Building
Grand Rapids, MI 49503
616-459-6281

VAC of Greater Kalamazoo
709-A Westnedge
Kalamazoo, MI 49007
616-382-8350

Voluntary Action Center of
Greater Lansing
6035 Executive Dr., Ste. 105
Lansing, MI 48911
517-887-8004

Voluntary Action Center of
Midland County, Inc.
220 W. Main St.
Midland, MI 48640
517-631-7660

Southwestern Michigan
Volunteer Center
1213 Oak St.
Niles, MI 49120
616-683-5464

Voluntary Action Center of
Saginaw County
100 S. Jefferson, 6th Fl.
Saginaw, MI 48607
517-755-2822

S.W. Michigan Volunteer Center
508 Pleasant St.
St. Joseph, MI 49085
616-983-0912

United Way of Monroe County
6 S. Monroe St.
Monroe, MI 48161
313-242-4357

Volunteer Center
of Isabella County
402 S. University
Mt. Pleasant, MI 48858
517-772-6194

Volunteer Center of Muskegon
161 Muskegon Mall, Ste. 610
Muskegon, MI 49440
616-727-8065

Volunteer Center of Kirtland Community College
(Roscommon, Crawford, Oscoda and Ogernaw Counties)
1077 N. St. Helen Rd.
Roscommon, MI 48653
517-275-5121

Grand Traverse Area Volunteer Center
United Way Community Services Bldg.
521 S. Union St.
P.O. Box 694
Traverse City, MI 49685
616-922-3566

Lenawee United Way and Volunteer Center
117 E. Maumee, Ste. 201
Adrian, MI 49221
517-263-4263

Albion Volunteer Service Center
(Albion, Concord, Homer, Parma, Springport)
203 S. Superior St.
Albion, MI 49224
517-629-5574

Community Volunteer Center
Mecosta-Osceola United Way
1302 E. Linden
Big Rapids, MI 49307
616-592-9800

Thumb Area Volunteer Center
429 Mantague Ave.
Caro, MI 48723
517-673-4121

Heart of West Michigan United Way
500 Commerce Building
Grand Rapids, MI 49503
616-459-6281

Volunteer Action Center of Keweenaw
801 N. Lincoln Dr., Rm. 204
Hancock, MI 49930
906-482-9930

Voluntary Action Center
Greater Holland United Way
70 W. 8th St.
P.O. Box 2363
Holland, MI 49423
616-396-7811

Volunteer Connection
Livingston County United Way
3780 E. Grand River
Howell, MI 48843
517-546-4612

N.M.U. Volunteer Center
P.O. Box 24
1401 Presque Isle
Marquette, MI 49855
906-227-2466

Marquette County Volunteer Referral Center
300 W. Baraga
Marquette, MI 49855
906-228-9111

Minnesota

Minnesota Office
on Volunteer Services
Dept. of Administration
117 University Ave.
St. Paul, MN 55155
612-296-4731

Minnesota Commission for
National & Community Service
683 Capitol Square Building
Saint Paul, MN 55101
612-296-1435

Voluntary Action Center of
United Way
424 W. Superior St., Ste. 402
Duluth, MN 55802
218-726-4776

United Way's Voluntary Center
404 S. 8th St.
Minneapolis, MN 55404
612-340-7621

The Volunteer Connection, Inc.
903 W. Center, Ste. 200
Rochester, MN 55902
507-287-2244

Voluntary Action Center
of the St. Paul Area, Inc.
251 Starkey St., Ste. 127
St. Paul, MN 55107
612-227-3938

Community Voluntary Service
of the St. Croix Valley
2300 Orleans St. W.
Stillwater, MN 55082
612-439-7434

Volunteer Services of
Carlton County, Inc.
1003 Cloquet Ave., Rm. 102
Cloquet, MN 55720
218-879-9238

The Volunteer Bridge
1230 Northwest School St.
Elk River, MN 55330
612-241-3520

Volunteer Center
P.O. Box 54
Fergus Falls, MN 56537
218-736-2856

Itasca County Voluntary
Action Center
Itasca Medical Center
126 Southeast 1st Ave.
Grand Rapids, MN 55744
218-326-7567

Hibbing Volunteer Council
P.O. Box 368
Hibbing, MN 55746
218-263-4493

The Volunteer Center of
Greater Mankato Area
929 N. 4th St.
Mankato, MN 56001
507-345-8888

Southwest Mentor Network/
Volunteer Center
University of MN Extension
Services
SS 109/SW State University
Marshall, MN 56258
507-537-6159

Volunteers in Action
Robinson High School
Resource Center
3730 Toledo Ave. N.
Robbinsdale, MN 55422
612-522-0293

United Way of St. Cloud Area's
Volunteer Connection Services
Corporate Centre, Ste. 20
26 N. 6th Ave.
P.O. Box 698
St. Cloud, MN 56302
612-252-0227

MAP for Nonprofits
2233 University Ave.
St. Paul, MN 55114
612-647-1216

Northland Volunteer Council, Inc.
801 9th St. N., Rm. 207
P.O. Box 570
Virginia, MN 55734

Volunteers Working Together
415 N. Jefferson, Rm. 203
Wadena, MN 56482
218-631-3510 ext. 321

Winona Volunteer Services, Inc.
71 E. Second St.
Winona, MN 55987
507-452-5591

Mississippi

Mississippi Commission for
National & Community Service
3825 Ridgewood Rd.
Jackson, MS 39211
601-982-6738

Volunteer Center of United Way
843 N. President St.
P.O. Box 23169
Jackson, MS 39225
601-354-1765

UW/Volunteer Center
3510 Magnolia St.
P.O. Box 97
Pascagoula, MS 39568
601-762-8557

Missouri

Missouri Commission
on Community Service
201 W. Capitol Ave., Rm. B-14B
Jefferson City, MO 65101
314-751-0382

Voluntary Action Center
800 N. Providence, Ste. 220
Columbia, MO 65201
314-874-2273

Voluntary Action Center of
Easter Jackson County
10901 Winner Rd., Ste. 102
Independence, MO 64052
816-252-2636

Volunteer Center—Heart of
America United Way
1080 Washington St.
Kansas City, MO 64105
816-474-5112

Voluntary Action Center
P.O. Box 188
St. Joseph, MO 64502
816-364-2381

United Way of
Greater St. Louis VAC
1111 Olive
St. Louis, MO 63101
314-421-0700

Montana

Montana Community Services
Advisory Council
State Capitol, Rm. 219
Helena, MT 59601
406-444-5547

United Way Student
Volunteer Program
600 Central Plaza, Ste. 327
Great Falls, MT 59401
406-727-3403

Nebraska

Nebraska Commission on
National & Community Service
State Capitol, 6th Fl., W. Side
Centennial Mall
Lincoln, NE 68509
402-471-6225

United Way of the Midlands
Volunteer Bureau/VAC
1805 Harney St.
Omaha, NE 68102
402-342-8232

Volunteer Center of
Scotts Bluff County
1721 Broadway, Rm. 409
Scottsbluff, NE 69361
308-632-3736

Nevada

Nevada Commission for
National & Community Service
1830 E. Sahara Ave., Ste. 314
Las Vegas, NV 89104
702-486-7997

United Way Services, Inc.
1660 E. Flamingo Rd.
Las Vegas, NV 89119
702-734-CARE

VAC/United Way of Northern
Nevada and the Sierra
1055 S. Wells Ave., Ste. 100
P.O. Box 2730
Reno, NV 89505
702-322-8668

New Hampshire

Governor's Office
on Volunteerism
25 Capitol St., Rm. 431
Concord, NH 03301
603-271-3771

New Hampshire Commission on
National & Community Service
64 Old Suncook Rd.
Concord, NH 03301
603-228-9500

Community Service Learning
New Hampshire
Dept. of Education
101 Pleasant St.
Concord, NH 03301
603-271-3719

Monadnock Volunteer Center
331 Main St.
Keene, NH 03431
603-352-2088

The Voluntary Action Center
102 N. Main St.
Manchester, NH 03431
603-668-8601

New Jersey

The Governor's Office
of Volunteerism
22 S. Warren CN 700
Trenton, NJ 08625
609-984-3470

New Jersey Commission on
National & Community Service
240 W. Broad St., CN 500
Trenton, NJ 08625
609-633-9629

Volunteer Center
of Hunterdon County
14 Route 31
Annadale, NJ 08801
908-735-4357

Volunteer Center of
Bergen County, Inc.
64 Passaic St.
Hackensack, NJ 07601
201-489-9454

United Way of Hudson County
857 Bergen Ave.
Jersey City, NJ 07306
201-434-2625

Greater Mercer Volunteer Center
3131 Princeton Pike, Bldg. 4
Lawrenceville, NJ 08648
609-896-1912

National Council of Jewish
Women
513 W. Mt. Pleasant Ave.
Livingston, NJ 07039
201-740-0588

Volunteer Services Center
32 Ford Ave.
P.O. Box 210
Milltown, NJ 08850
908-247-3727

Volunteers of Morris County
280 W. Hanover Ave.
Morristown, NJ 07960
201-538-7200

Volunteer Center
of Atlantic County
P.O. Box 648
Northfield, NJ 08225
609-272-2488

Volunteer Center
of Greater Essex
439 Main St., Rm. 200
Orange, NJ 07050
201-676-8899

United Way of Passaic County
22 Mill St., 3rd Fl.
Paterson, NJ 07501
201-279-8900

Volunteer Center
of Monmouth County
227 E. Bergen Place
Red Bank, NJ 07701
201-741-3330

Volunteer Center
of Somerset County
United Way of Somerset County
205 W. Main St.
Somerville, NJ 08876
908-725-6640

Volunteer Center
of Warren County
P.O. Box 418
Washington, NJ 07882
908-689-2755

New Mexico

New Mexico Commission for
National & Community Service
Children Youth and Family Dept.
300 San Mateo SE, Ste. 500
Albuquerque, NM 87103
505-841-2983

The Volunteer Center
of Albuquerque
302 8th St. NW
P.O. Box 1767
Albuquerque, NM 87103
505-247-3671

New York

New York Commission on
National & Community Service
Executive Chamber—State
Capitol
Albany, NY 12224
518-473-8882

The Volunteer Center
of Albany, Inc.
100 State St.
Albany, NY 12207
518-434-2061

Voluntary Action Center
of Broome County
Vestal Pkwy. E. at Jensen Rd.
P.O. Box 550
Binghamton, NY 13902
607-729-2592

Volunteer Center of the United
Way of Buffalo/Erie Counties
742 Delaware Ave.
Buffalo, NY 14209
716-887-2632

The Volunteer Connection
29 Denison Pkwy E., Ste. A
Corning, NY 14830
607-936-3753

VAC of Greater Glens Falls, Inc.
65 Ridge St.
Glens Falls, NY 12801
516-793-3817

Volunteer Service Bureau
of S. Chautauqua County
P.O. Box 1012
Jamestown, NY 14701
716-483-1562

Long Island Volunteer Center
264 Old Country Rd.
Mineola, NY 11501
516-294-5482

Mayor's Voluntary Action Center
61 Chambers St.
New York, NY 10007
212-788-7550

Volunteer Action Center
27 W. Main St.
Norwich, NY 13815
607-334-8815

United Way
Volunteer Action Center
59 Church St.
P.O. Box 235
Owego, NY 13827
607-887-4082

Volunteer Center of
Dutchess County
9 Vassar St.
Poughkeepsie, NY 12603
914-452-5600

Volunteer Resources Division
55 St. Paul St.
Rochester, NY 14604
716-454-2770

Rome Voluntary Action Center
327 W. Thomas St.
Rome, NY 13440
315-336-5638

Volunteer Center, Inc. of
Syracuse & Onondaga County
115 E. Jefferson St., Ste. 400
Syracuse, NY 13202
315-474-7011

Volunteer Center
of Rensselaer County
272 River St.
Troy, NY 12180
518-272-1000

Voluntary Action Center of
Greater Utica, Inc.
1644 Genesee St.
Utica, NY 13502
315-735-4463

Volunteer Center
of Jefferson County
37 Empsall Plaza
Watertown, NY 13601
315-788-5631

Volunteer Center of United Way
470 Mamaroneck Ave., Rm. 204
White Plains, NY 10605
914-948-4452

North Carolina

Governor's Office of Volunteerism
116 W. Jones St.
Raleigh, NC 27603
919-733-2391

The Volunteer Center
c/o United Way of Asheville
& Buncombe County
50 S. French Broad Ave.
Asheville, NC 28801
704-255-0696

Moore County Volunteer Center
P.O. Box 905
Carthage, NC 28327
910-947-6395

The Volunteer Center
P.O. Box 845
Chapel Hill, NC 27514
919-929-7273

The Volunteer Center
301 S. Brevard St.
Charlotte, NC 28202
704-372-7170

Volunteer Center of
Greater Durham, Inc.
136 E. Chapel Hill St.
Durham, NC 27701
919-688-8977

Volunteer Center
P.O. Box 2001
Fayetteville, NC 28302
910-323-8643

The Volunteer Center
of Greensboro
1500 Yanceyville St.
Greensboro, NC 27405
910-373-1633

Volunteer Center
of Vance County, Inc.
215 S. Garnett St.
P.O. Box 37
Henderson, NC 27536
919-492-1540

United Way of Wake County
Voluntary Action Center
1100 Wake Forest Rd.
P.O. Box 11426
Raleigh, NC 27604
919-833-5739

United Way of
Cleveland County, Inc.
132 W. Graham St.
P.O. Box 2242
Shelby, NC 28151
704-482-7344

Volunteer Center—United Way
400 W. 4th St.
P.O. Box 20669-27120
Winston-Salem, NC 27101
910-723-3601

North Dakota

Missouri Slope Areawide
United Way
P.O. Box 2111
Bismarck, ND 58502
701-255-3601

United Way of Cass-Clay
315 N. 8th St.
P.O. Box 1609
Fargo, ND 58107
701-237-5050

United Way Volunteer Center
406 DeMers Ave.
Grand Forks, ND 58201
701-775-0671

Ohio

Governor's Community Service
Commission
51 N. High St., Ste. 481
Columbus, OH 43215
614-728-2916

Volunteer Ohio
1335 Dublin Rd., Ste. 126 D
Columbus, OH 43215
614-227-9080

The Volunteer Center
425 W. Market St.
Akron, OH 44302
216-762-8991

Voluntary Action Center/
A Service of United Way
618 Second St. NW
Canton, OH 44703
216-453-9172

Info-Line/Volunteer Bureau
107 Water St.
Chardon, OH 44024
216-729-7931

VAC/United Appeal &
Community Chest
2400 Reading Rd.
Cincinnati, OH 45202
513-762-7192

First Link, Inc.
370 S. 5th Ave.
Columbus, OH 43215
614-221-6766

Voluntary Action Center of United
Way/Greater Dayton Area
184 Salem Ave.
Dayton, OH 45406
513-225-3066

United Way of
Hancock County VAC
124 W. Front St.
Findlay, OH 45840
419-423-1775

The Voluntary Action
Center of Lorain County
1875 N. Ridge Rd. E., Ste. H
Lorain, OH 44055
216-277-6530

Vinton Area Ministry
202 W. High St.
McArthur, OH 45651
614-596-5562

The Volunteer Center
of Richland County
35 N. Park St.
Mansfield, OH 44902
419-525-2816

Medina County United Way
Volunteer Center
113 E. Homestead St.
Medina, OH 44256
216-725-3926

Middletown Area United Way
29 City Centre Plaza
Middletown, OH 45042
513-423-9761

The Volunteer Center
in Huron County
Shady Lane Complex #4
258 Benedict Ave.
Norwalk, OH 44857
419-663-1179

The Volunteer Center
108 W. Shoreline Dr.
Sandusky, OH 44870
419-627-0074

Volunteer Service Bureau
616 N. Limestone St.
Springfield, OH 45503
513-322-4262

United Way/Voluntary
Action Center
1 Stranahan Square, Ste. 114
Toledo, OH 43604
419-244-3063

United Way/W.H.I.R.E.
215 S. Walnut St.
Wooster, OH 44691
216-264-9473

The Volunteer Center of
Youngstown/Mohoning Valley
5500 Market St., Ste. 106
Youngstown, OH 44512
216-782-1220

Oklahoma

The Governor's Commission
for Community Service
1515 N. Lincoln
Oklahoma City, OK 73104
405-235-7278

The Volunteer Center
of Muskogee
5319 Emporia Ave.
Muskogee, OK 74402
918-682-1365

Tulsa Volunteer Center
1430 S. Boulder
Tulsa, OK 74119
918-585-5551

Oregon

Oregon Community Service Commission
Portland State University
491 Newburger
Portland, OR 97207
503-725-5903

UW/Volunteer Connection
123 Oakway Center
Eugene, OR 97401
503-484-6666

The Volunteer Center
619 SW 11th Ave.
Portland, OR 97205
503-222-1355

Pennsylvania

PennSERVE
The Governor's Office of Citizen Service
Dept. of Labor & Industry
1304 Labor & Industry Building
Harrisburg, PA 17120
717-787-1971

United Way SEPA
Volunteer Centers
Neumann College
Aston, PA 19014
610-558-5639

Voluntary Action Center
of the United Way
520 E. Broad St.
P.O. Box 6478
Bethlehem, PA 18018
215-691-6670

GUIDELINE
520 Rush St.
P.O. Box 8
Blossburg, PA 16912
800-332-6718

Volunteer Center
of Clearfield County
103 N. Front St.
P.O. Box 550
Clearfield, PA 16830
814-765-1398

Volunteer Services
110 W. 10th St.
Erie, PA 16501
814-456-2937

The Volunteer Center
546 Maclay St.
Harrisburg, PA 17110
717-238-6678

Volunteer Center
of Lancaster County
630 Janet Ave.
Lancaster, PA 17601
717-299-3743

United Way SEPA
Volunteer Centers
7 Benjamin Franklin Pkwy.
Philadelphia, PA 19103
215-665-2474

Volunteer Action Center
United Way
of Allegheny County
P.O. Box 735
Pittsburgh, PA 15230
412-456-6880

Volunteer Action Center
Associate, JCCEOA Inc.
Mill Creek Center
105 Grace Way
Punxsutawney, PA 15767
814-938-3302

Volunteer Center/UW
of Berks County
P.O. Box 302
501 Washington St.
Reading, PA 19603
215-371-4571

Voluntary Action Center
Scranton Life Building
538 Spruce St.
Scranton, PA 18503
717-347-5616

OHR
Box 396
Selinsgrove, PA 17870
717-374-0181

Voluntary Action Center of
Centre County, Inc.
1524 W. College Ave.
State College, PA 16801
814-234-8222

VAC of Wyoming Valley
United Way of Wyoming Valley
9 E. Market St.
Wilkes-Barre, PA 18711
717-822-3020

The Volunteer Center
of York County
800 E. King St.
York, PA 17403
717-846-4477

Puerto Rico

Puerto Rico State Commission
of Community Service
La Fortaleza
San Juan, PR 00901
809-721-7877

Rhode Island

Rhode Island Commission for
National & Community Service
903 Broad St.
Providence, RI 02907
401-461-6305

Volunteers in Action
168 Broad St.
Providence, RI 02903
401-421-6547

South Carolina

Division of Volunteer Service
of the Governor's Office
1205 Pendleton St., Ste. 405
Columbia, SC 29201
803-734-1677

Western Foothills United Way
Volunteer Center
114 W. Greenville St.
P.O. Box 2067
Anderson, SC 29622
803-226-1078

Volunteer & Info Center
of Beaufort
2732 Boundary
P.O. Box 202
Beaufort, SC 29901
803-524-4357

VAC-Trident United Way
P.O. Box 20696
Charleston, SC 29413
803-723-5000

United Way of the Midlands
1800 Main St.
P.O. Box 152
Columbia, SC 29202
803-733-5400

Volunteer Greenville—
A Volunteer Center
301 University Ridge, Ste. 5300
Greenville, SC 29601
803-467-3330

Voluntary Action Center
20 Palmetto Pkwy., Ste. 106
Hilton Head Island, SC 29926
803-681-7811

Oconee Volunteer &
Information Services
P.O. Box 1694
Seneca, SC 29679
803-882-9743

United Way of the Piedmont
Volunteer Center
P.O. Box 5624
Spartanburg, SC 29304
803-582-7556

Volunteer Sumter, Inc.
P.O. Box 957
Sumter, SC 29151
803-775-9424

South Dakota

Governor's Office
Special Assistant to the
Governor for Volunteerism
500 E. Capital Ave.
Pierre, SD 57501
605-773-3661

Volunteer & Information Center
1321 W. 22nd St.
Sioux Falls, SD 57105
605-339-4357

Tennessee

Tennessee Commission for
National & Community Service
302 John Sevier Building
500 Charlotte Ave.
Nashville, TN 37243
615-532-9250

The Volunteer Center of
Chattanooga & the
Tri-state Area
406 Fraizer Ave.
P.O. Box 4070
Chattanooga, TN 37405
615-265-0514

Volunteer-Johnson City, Inc.
200 E. Main
P.O. Box 1443
Johnson City, TN 37605
615-926-8010

Volunteer ETSU
Student Activities Center
E. Tennessee State
Johnson City, TN 37614
615-929-4254

Volunteer Kingsport, Inc.
1701 Virginia Ave., Ste. 17
Kingsport, TN 37664
615-247-4511

Volunteer Center
of Greater Knoxville
1514 E. 5th Ave.
P.O. Box 326
Knoxville, TN 37901
615-521-0890

Volunteer Center of Memphis
326 Eltsworth
Memphis, TN 38111
901-458-3288

Volunteer Center-United Way
of Middle Nashville
P.O. Box 24667
Nashville, TN 37202
615-256-8272

Texas

Texas Commission for National
& Community Service
Sam Houston Building
201 E. 14th St., Ste. 680
Austin, TX 78701
512-463-1814

Volunteer Center of Abilene, Inc.
P.O. Box 3953
Abilene, TX 79604
915-676-5683

United Way Volunteer
Action Center
200 S. Tyler St.
Amarillo, TX 79101
806-373-2652

United Way of Brazoria County
P.O. Box 1959
Angelton, TX 77516
409-849-4404

Capital Area Volunteer
Center, Inc.
105 W. Riverside Dr., Ste. 233
Austin, TX 78704
512-346-1313

Volunteer Center
of the Coastal Bend
3164 Reid Dr., Ste. 202
Corpus Christi, TX 78404
512-855-3500

Volunteer Center of Dallas County
1215 Skiles
Dallas, TX 75204
214-826-6767

Center for Volunteerism
103 Montana, Ste. 307
El Paso, TX 79902
915-534-3441

Volunteer Center of
Metropolitan Tarrant County
210 E. 9th St.
Ft. Worth, TX 76102
817-878-0099

The Volunteer Center
of the Texas Gulf Coast
3100 Timmons Lane, Ste. 100
Houston, TX 77027
713-965-0031

Volunteer Center of Lubbock
1706 23rd St., Ste. 101
Lubbock, TX 79411
806-747-0551

The Nonprofit Resource Center
P.O. Box 2145
Midland, TX 79702
915-697-8781

Volunteer Center of Collin County
301 W. Parker Rd., Ste. 213
Plano, TX 75023
214-422-1050

Round Rock Volunteer Center
216 E. Main St.
Round Rock, TX 78664
512-388-4575

UW of San Antonio
& Bexar County
700 S. Alamo
P.O. Box 898
San Antonio, TX 78293
512-224-5000

Texarkana Volunteer Center
3000 Texas Blvd.
Texarkana, TX 75503
903-793-4903

Volunteer Center of Tyler
P.O. Box 130428
Tyler, TX 75713
903-592-7318

Volunteer Connection
5400 Bosque Blvd.
Waco, TX 76710
817-741-1980

Utah

Utah Commission on National
& Community Service
324 S. State St., Ste. 240
Salt Lake City, UT 84114
801-538-8611

United Way of Davis County
45 W. 200 S.
Bountiful, UT 84010
801-295-6677

Volunteeer Center of Cache Valley
236 N. 100 E.
P.O. Box 567
Logan, UT 84321
801-752-3103

Weber County Volunteer Services
2650 Lincoln Ave., Rm. 268
Ogden, UT 84401
801-625-3782

United Way Volunteer Center
148 N. 100 W.
P.O. Box 135
Provo, UT 84603
801-374-8108

The Volunteer Center
1025 S. 700 W.
Salt Lake City, UT 84104
801-978-2452

Vermont

Vermont Governor's
Commission on Volunteerism
63 Central St.
Northfield, VT 05663
802-828-8803

Vermont Commission on
National & Community Service
Governor's Office, Pavillion
Office Building
133 State St.
Montpelier, VT 05633
802-828-4982

Volunteer Connection
95 St. Paul St.
Burlington, VT 05401
802-864-7498

Virginia

Virginia Department
of Volunteerism
730 E. Broad St., 9th Fl.
Richmond, VA 23219
804-692-1950

Alexandria Volunteer Bureau
2210 Mt. Vernon Ave.
Alexandria, VA 22301
703-836-2176

The Arlington Volunteer Office
2100 Clarendon Blvd.
#1 Court House Plaza, Ste. 314
Arlington, VA 22201
703-358-3222

Volunteer Action Center of
Montgomery County
Corner of W. Roanoke
and Otey Streets
P.O. Box 565
Blacksburg, VA 24063
703-552-4909

Volunteer-Bristol
600 Cumberland St.
Second Floor
Bristol, VA 24201
703-669-1555

United Way Volunteer Services
413 E. Market
P.O. Box 139
Charlottesville, VA 22902
804-972-1705

Volunteer Center
of Fairfax County
10530 Page Ave.
Fairfax, VA 22030
703-246-3460

Voluntary Action Center
of the United Way
1520 Alberdeen Rd., Ste. 109
Hampton, VA 23666
804-838-9770

Volunteer Services
of Hanover County
P.O. Box 470
Hanover, VA 23069
804-798-0896

VAC of United Way
of Central Virginia
1010 Miller Park Square
P.O. Box 2434
Lynchburg, VA 24501
804-847-8657

VAC of the Prince William
Area, Inc.
9300 Peabody St., Ste. 108
Manassas, VA 22110
703-369-5292

VAC of S. Hampton Roads
100 E. Main St.
Norfolk, VA 23510
804-624-2403

Volunteer Center/United Way
Services
233 S. Adam St.
P.O. Box 227
Petersburg, VA 23804
804-861-9330

Volunteer Center
224 E. Broad St.
P.O. Box 12209
Richmond, VA 23241
804-771-5855

Voluntary Action Center
502 Campbell Ave. SW
Roanoke, VA 24016
703-985-0131

Washington

Washington State Center
for Voluntary Action
9th and Columbia Building
MS-8300
Olympia, WA 98504
206-753-9684

Washington Commission on
National & Community Service
Insurance Building, Rm. 100
#43113
Olympia, WA 98504
206-586-8292

Volunteer Center of American
Red Cross
2111 King St.
Bellingham, WA 98225
206-733-3290

United Way of Snohomish
County's Volunteer Center
917 134th St. SW, A-6
Everett, WA 98204
206-742-5911

Benton-Franklin Volunteer
Center
205 N. Dennis
Kennewick, WA 99336
509-783-0631

Voluntary Action Center
613-S Second
P.O. Box 1507
Mt. Vernon, WA 98273
206-336-6627

Center for Volunteerism and
Citizen Services
908 Columbia St. SW
Olympia, WA 98504
206-753-9684

United Way Volunteer Center
of King County
107 Cherry St., 7th Fl.
Seattle, WA 98104
206-461-4539

United Way's Volunteer Center
P.O. Box 326
Spokane, WA 99210
509-624-2279

United Way of Pierce County
734 Broadway
P.O. Box 2215
Tacoma, WA 98401
206-272-4267

Volunteer Center of Clark County
1703 Main St.
P.O. Box 425
Vancouver, WA 98666
206-694-6577

West Virginia

West Virginia Commission for
National & Community Service
Route 2, Box 51 A
Walker, WV 26180
304-679-3970

Kanawha Valley Volunteer
Action Center
One United Way Square
Charleston, WV 25301
304-340-3526

Volunteer Action Center
P.O. Box 777
Parkersburg, WV 26102
304-422-8508

Wisconsin

Wisconsin National and
Community Service Board
101 E. Wilson St., 6th Fl.
Madison, WI 53702
608-266-8234

Volunteer Center
338 S. Chestnut
Green Bay, WI 54303
414-435-1101

Kenosha Voluntary Action
Center of Kenosha, Inc.
716 58th St.
Kenosha, WI 53140
414-657-4554

United Way Voluntary
Action Center
P.O. Box 7548
Madison, WI 53707
608-246-4380

Volunteer Center of Ozaukee
N. 143 W. 6515 Pioneer Rd.
Cedarburg, WI 53012
414-377-1616

Volunteer Center of Greater
Milwaukee, Inc.
600 E. Mason St., Ste. 100
Milwaukee, WI 53202
414-273-7887

Volunteer Center of Waukesha
County, Inc.
2220 Silvernail Rd.
Pewaukee, WI 53072
414-544-0150

The Volunteer Center
of Marathon County
407 Grant St.
Wausau, WI 54401
715-843-1220

Volunteer Center of
Washington County
120 N. Main St., #340
West Bend, WI 53095
414-338-8256

United Way of S. Wood County
Volunteer Center
1120 Lincoln St., Ste. 2
Wisconsin Rapids, WI 54494
715-421-0390

Wyoming

Wyoming Commission for
National & Community Service
Herschler Building, 4th Fl. E.
Cheyenne, WY 82002
307-777-5396

Volunteer Information Center
900 Central
P.O. Box 404
Cheyenne, WY 82003
307-632-4132

About the Author

Theresa Foy DiGeronimo is a highly acclaimed author of 20 nonfiction books. Two of her books for teens have been honored by the New York Public Library System and are included in its recommended reading list. As a high school and college English teacher, DiGeronimo has worked closely with young adults for many years. Currently she is busy teaching, writing and raising her three children in Hawthorne, New Jersey.

About the Author

Index

A Student's Guide to Volunteering

Adult tutoring, 70-71
AIDS, 23, 126
Air pollution, 82
Alzheimer's, 25
American Cancer Society, 10
American Hospital Association, 25
American Red Cross, the, 26, 54
AmeriCorps, 125-126
Assistance to hospital staff, 21

Beach, Veronica, 37
Boredom, relieving, 13
Boy Scouts, 10
Boys and Girls Clubs, 10, 72
Building credentials, 12

Camp Lots of Fun, 55
Candystriper, uniforms, 23
Canvassing, for political campaigns, 100
CARE, 54
Career experience, gaining, 12-13
Castlewood Public Library, 121
Center for Substance Abuse Prevention, 33, 38
Challenge, desire for, 14
Christmas in April USA, 51
Citizen's Alcohol and Other Drug Prevention Directory: Resources for Getting Involved, 43
Citizens for Recycling and Usage of Disposables (CRUD), 11
Civil War, volunteering during the, 10
Clerical work, for political campaigns, 101
Clinton, Bill, 125
Colonial American period, volunteering during, 10
Common sense, 15
Community for Automobile Responsibility and Safety (CARS), 38

Compassion, 15, 18
Confidentiality, 19, 35-36
Credentials, building, 12
Crime Watch, 103

Defenders of Wildlife, 84
Department of Education, 70
Depression, volunteering during the, 10
Disabled, helping the, 126
Disaster victims, helping, 54
Drinking water pollution, 82
Driving under the influence of drugs or alcohol, 36-38
Education volunteering, 63-77
  adult tutoring, 70-71
  behavior and appearance, 72
  benefits, 74
  commitment, 64
  helping inner-city children, 66-67
  helping religious groups, 69-70
  helping the functionally illiterate, 65-66
  immigrant tutoring, 71
  peer counseling, 67-68
  peer tutoring, 67
  qualifications, 64-65
  reasons for, 63-64
  tutoring younger kids, 68-69
Energy conservation projects, 86
Enthusiasm, 14
Environmental Protection Agency, 82
Environmental protection volunteering, 79-94
  career possibilities, 81
  characteristics needed, 87
  commitment, 88-89
  fields of concern, 81-82
  hands-on involvement, 86-88
  lobbying, 83
  office work, 83-84
  reasons for, 80
  starting a group, 89
  teaching others, 84-86
Ethics, code of, 19
Experience, gaining career, 12-13

Food for the Hungry, 54
Forest and tree preservation, 82
Forshay, Mike, 58-61
Friends of the Library, 120
Functionally illiterate, helping, 65-66
Fund raising, for political campaigns, 100
Future Educators of America, 68

Global problems, 82
Goodwill Industries, 10
Greenhouse effect, 82
Greenpeace USA, 84, 118

Habitat for Humanity International, 51
Health care volunteering, 17-32
  assistance to hospital staff, 21

clinics or rehabilitation centers, 26
confidentiality, 19
for medical career, 18
for nursing career, 17
getting started, 25-26
patient contact assignments, 20
reasons for, 17-18
requirements for, 18-19
services to visitors, 20-21
Health requirements, 19
Help and Information Resource (HAIR), 11
Helping disaster victims, 54
Helping inner-city children, 66-67
Helping religious groups, 69-70
Helping the disabled, 126
Helping the functionally illiterate, 65-66
Helping the homeless, 51-52
Helping the illiterate, 53-54
Helping the poor, 52-53
Hepatitis B, 23
History of volunteering, 10
HIV/AIDS, 23
Homeless, helping the, 51-52
Hospital volunteering, 19-21
admitting, 20
appearance, 24
assistance to staff, 21
behavior, 22
childcare center, 21
clerical, 21
dietary, 20
hospitality gift cart, 20
laboratory, 21
mail and flower delivery, 20
mailroom, 21
nursing units, 20
radiology host or hostess, 20
recognition and awards, 24-25
recovery room, 20
safety precautions, 22-23
services to visitors, 20
sewing room, 21
time commitment, 21
training, 22
transport, 20
uniforms, 23
"How to Start Your SADD Chapter and New Ideas for Existing SADD Chapters," 37

Illiterate, helping the, 53-54
Immigrant tutoring, 71
Ingenuity, 15
Inner-city children, helping, 66-67
Inoculations, 19
Interests, sharing, 13

Just Say No program, 38-39

Key Club, the, 66
Kids Against Pollution (KAP), 85
Kids To Kids, 84

Legal Action Center for the Homeless, 52
Lincoln, Abraham, 99
Lions Club, the, 85, 120
Literacy Volunteers of America, 71

Litter control/cleanup, 86
Lobbying, 83

March of Dimes, the, 26
Meals on Wheels, 103
Medicine, 18
Meeting people, 13
Metro-help, 11
Mothers Against Drunk Driving (MADD), 36-37
Municipal Alliance Committee, 119

National and Community Service Act, 125
National Assessment of Educational Progress, 70
National Association for Mental Health, the, 10
National Audubon Society, 87
National Clearinghouse for Alcohol and Drug Information, 43
National Coalition for the Homeless, 55
National Commission on Excellence in Education, 65
National Council on Alcoholism and Drug Dependence (NCADD), 41
National Geographic World, 11
National Highway Traffic Safety Administration, 38
National Honor Society, 67
National Multiple Sclerosis Society, the, 26
National organizations, for substance abuse prevention, 41
National Society for the Prevention of Blindness, the, 10
National Student Campaign Against Hunger and Homelessness, 55
National Tuberculosis Association, the, 10
Natural Guard, the, 88
Natural resources, preservation of, 82
Nature preserves, preservation of, 86
Needy volunteering, 49-61
    getting started, 55-56
    helping disaster victims, 54
    helping the homeless, 51-52
    helping the illiterate, 53-54
    helping the poor, 52-53
    reasons for, 49-50
    recognition/rewards, 56-57
    requirements, 50-51
    school-based groups, 54-55
    summer camp, 55
Neighborhood Watch, 103
Newsweek, 11
1960's, volunteering during, 10
Nursing, 17

Operation Cork, 38
Ozone depletion, 82

Patient contact assignments, 20
Peer counseling, 39, 67-68

Peer tutoring, 67
Personal interest, sharing, 13
Phi Delta Kappan, 11
Poliquin, Ron, 105-107
Political volunteering, 95-107
  characteristics needed, 96-99
  for election campaigns, 99-102
  for political parties, 102-103
  getting started, 104
  reasons for, 96
Pollution site identification, 87
Pollution
  air, 82
  of drinking water, 82
  of rivers, streams and oceans, 81
Poor, helping the, 52-53
Preservation of natural resources, 82
Preservation of nature preserves, 86
Privacy
  of patients, 19
  of substance abusers, 35-36
Project Interact, 57
Protecting the environment, 79-94

Reading is Fundamental, 66
Recycling projects, 86
Red Cross, the, 10
Religious groups, helping, 69-70
Remove Intoxicated Drivers (RID), 37-38
Republican Committee, 106
River, stream and ocean pollution, 81
Roberts' Rules of Order, 115
Romanick, John, 75-77
Roosevelt, Franklin Delano, 99
Rotary, the, 85, 120

Saferides, 35, 42
Salvation Army, the, 10, 56, 59
Save A Tree organization, 82
School requirements, fulfilling, 13-14
Services to visitors, 20-21
Sober drivers, 36
Special Olympics, the, 75-76
Starting your own organization
  adult supervision, 112
  brainstorming, 116
  creating an Action Plan, 117
  help from friends, 110-111
  information gathering, 110
  meeting place, 111-112
  meeting time, 111
  preparing for your first meeting, 113-116
  raising money, 119-120, 124
  recruiting members, 112-113
Storm drain stenciling, 87
Student Conservation Association, Inc., 11, 88-89
Student Council, 67
Students Against Driving Drunk (SADD), 36-37, 40, 103, 120
Students of Hawthorne Acting Responsibly and Effectively (SHARE), 11
Substance abuse prevention volunteering
  appearance, 41
  common tasks, 41
  confidentiality, 35-36

getting started, 43
national organizations, 41
peer counseling, 39
reasons for, 34
requirements, 34-35
rewards and recognition, 42
starting a program, 38
time commitment, 41
Substance Abuse
Prevention, 33-47

Team spirit, 15
Teenage Republicans, 97, 101, 103-107
Time, 11
Together Getting Into Focus (TGIF), 44
Touch America Project, 87
Tree planting, 86
Tropical rain forest destruction, 82
Tutoring younger kids, 68-69

U.S. Bureau of Census, 52
U.S. Department of Agriculture Forest Service, 87
U.S. News & World Report, 11

Van Hise, Tracy, 90-94
Volunteer organization, starting your own, 109-124
Volunteering
education, 63-77
environmental protection, 79-94
for the needy, 49-61
history of, 10
in health care, 17-32
in politics, 95-107
reasons for, 12-14
substance abuse prevention, 33-47
Volunteers in Service to Education (VISTE), 68
Volunteers
characteristics of, 11-12
personality of, 14-15

Water pollution, 81-82
Waterway protection, 87
Wildlife, 81
World War I, 10

Young Democrats, 96, 103
Young Men's Christian Association (YMCA), 10, 66, 72
Youth Elderly Services (YES), 11
Youth Power training program, 39